Get Plugged In!

Harnessing The Power of Social Media and Online Marketing

Ronke Jegede

Published by: JIL Publishing, London, UK

ISBN NO 978-0-9934509-3-8

First Edition Printed in UK

Disclaimer

This book is written in two parts: the first part is on social media marketing and the second part is about online marketing and advertisement. While the first part is divided into chapters, the second part is divided into sections. This book (both parts) is published for information purpose only. Written as accurately as possible, this book is meant to be used as a guide and not as an ultimate source or authority. The information provided herewith are accurate only up to the date of publishing.

Though there may be some typographical errors or mistakes in content, this book is written for the sole purpose of educating and equipping the reader. The author and publisher does not warrant that the content of this book is whole in totality and thus shall not be responsible for any error in omission or whatsoever. The author and publisher shall have neither liability nor responsibility to any individual or entity with respect to any loss or damage caused or alleged to be caused directly or otherwise by this book.

Table of Contents

Introduction

That the advent and advancement of the internet has changed the course of the world's business strategy is no news. More so is the extensive development and utilisation of social media platforms like Facebook, Twitter, Google+, Instagram and a host of others. Maximising these social media platform is a sure way (if not the only way), to grow your business, build your reputation and boost your sales (and therefore profit) in a very short period of time.

This book will attempt to take you by the hand and walk you through all you have to know and do, to put your business in the vanguard of your niche or industry, using social media platform that is free and available at the tip of your fingers.

In this book, you will learn the following:-

- How to set up your accounts and pages on these platforms.
- The kind of content to create that will attract your prospective customers and make them stay on your platform.
- How to use the various services available online to automate your posts across all your social media accounts so that you will spend less time working on your social media network and more time on the content and other more important issues that will grow your business.

These strategies when implemented and followed diligently will eventually boost your online presence. So get your reading glasses on, and get set to shoot your business to the top.

Chapter 1

Social Media Defined

Social Media is clearly a form of communication tool that can be used to converse and interact with people, engage and work with people, teach and instruct and also bring some kind of entertainment.

Andreas M. Kaplan, Professor of Marketing and Communications at ESCP Europe and Michael Haenlein, Professor of Marketing at the business school ESCP Europe have defined social media as "a group of Internet-based applications that build on the ideological and technological foundations of Web 2.0, and that allow the creation and exchange of user-generated content."(1)

According to Wikipedia "social media are computer-mediated tools that enable people to create, share or exchange information, ideas, and pictures/videos in virtual communities and networks." (2)

Social media has evolved into an obsession and almost a way of life in this digital age. It has undoubtedly altered the way people communicate with their loved ones, colleagues, favourite brands and also impacted businesses.

As social media keeps on advancing in almost every area, the idea that social media is "just a fad" is no longer the notion, as more and more demographics move toward utilising social media on a daily basis. Social media has been the recipient of exponential growth in the last ten years; this is an obvious sign that more people are opting to use social networks to connect and communicate.

REFERENCES

(1)Andreas M. Kaplan and Michael Haenlein (2010), "Users of the world, unite! The challenges and opportunities of social media," Business Horizons 53 (1): 59-68.

(2)http://en.wikipedia.org/wiki/Social_media

Chapter 2

Forms of Social Media

There are numerous types of online platforms categorised under the large canopy of social media. These categories include:

Blogs, micro-blogs, social networking sites, video-sharing sites, photo-sharing sites, instant messaging, wikis, podcasts, virtual worlds, widgets and more.

Blogs: This is short for "weblog." Blogs are the most popular types of social media and they have been around for the longest. A blog is an online journal, the contents written on pages are called posts and the posts tend to be displayed in reverse chronological order (the most recent post appears first). Most blogs are interactive; people who visit the blog can make comments on such posts.

Micro-blogs: The main feature of a microblog is that you can only upload short posts. Users are typically limited to posting a few lines of text, unlike a typical blog which does not restrict the content that that can be posted. Microblogging is very popular for posting quick updates, Twitter and Tumblr are prominent microblogging sites. Users of microblogging sites can also upload images and videos.

Social networking sites: These websites allow users to set up web pages containing personal profiles ranging from their interests, pictures, videos and various other posts. These platforms are used to make connections with family, friends, colleagues and other users. There are a number of popular social networking sites in existence these days; this includes Facebook, LinkedIn, Twitter, Instagram and Pinterest to mention a few.

Video sharing sites: This was defined by the PC Mag as "a website that lets people upload and share their video clips with the public at large or to invited guests". (1) Viddler, Vimeo and YouTube are examples of video sharing sites, YouTube is however the biggest video sharing site.

Media sharing sites: Such sites are often freemium based, providing a modest amount of free storage and paid subscriptions for greater storage. A lot of such websites have extra features that would enable them to leave comments for instance. Flickr is an example of a media sharing sites.

Wikis: This is a communal website where any contributor can create content on the site. Although a wiki is a type of content management system, it is entirely different from a typical website or blog because the contents are created by anyone who wants to contribute not just the person or persons who set up the site. One of the popular wikis is Wikipedia.

Social bookmarking sites: "Social bookmarking is a user-defined taxonomy system for bookmarks". (2) Classic examples are Del.cio.us, Digg, Reddit and StumbleUpon and Digg.

Status-update services: These are also known as microblogging services and they provide users the platform where they can share short updates about anything and also view updates created by others.

Virtual world: These websites provide game-like virtual environments where users are able to interact with each other. A good example of such a site is secondlife.com.

Podcasts: According to Merriam-Webster, a podcast is "a program (as of music or talk) made available in digital format for automatic download over the Internet." (3) Podcasts are audio and video files and are often listened to on portable media players.

There are other forms of social media such as:

Rating and review sites (e.g. Yelp)

Forums and discussion boards (such as Yahoo Answers)
Music and audio sharing (e.g. Spotify; Pandora Radio)

Key Social Media Platforms

There are at least seven social media platforms that businesses should be on and they are as follows:-

Facebook
Twitter
YouTube
Linkedin
Instagram
Pinterest
Blogs

REFERENCES

(1) http://www.pcmag.com/encyclopedia/term/57378/video-sharing-site
(2) http://whatis.techtarget.com/definition/social-bookmarking
(3) https://www.merriam-webster.com/dictionary/podcast

Chapter 3

Benefits of Social Media for Businesses

The are numerous benefits of using social media for business, a few have been highlighted below:-

Making connections

Social media is definitely an excellent way to make connections with people who are usually hard to engage or hard-to-reach. Communicating with them on social media somehow helps to remove the barriers.

Build awareness of your business

Additionally, you can use social media to build awareness of your business, what you have to offer and what you believe. While your website may do the same thing, the reality is that people are not likely to just stumble across your site and take it all in. They'd have to be searching for it in the first place. However, with social media, your message can just show up in front of people who probably aren't searching for it, but might be receptive to it, especially when the message arrives via a trusted friend, colleague or family member.

It can be an effort multiplier

Although social media does have the potential to be impersonal, it also is, however, a great channel for informal, casual interactions — just the type of communication that can lead to more substantive discussions later on. Imagine being able to have many of these initial interactions and more of them without leaving your chair (not that it is a good idea to suggest not getting out and meeting people personally). Or imagine spreading a message to a variety of audiences all at once or a tool where people who hear about your business, can then each quickly spread word about your business to their friends and family with only the click of a mouse!

How else could you simultaneously advertise your business to disparate groups of people? Where can you can send a message or piece of content once, without having to repeat it for group 1, group 2, then group 3 and so on?

Businesses cannot afford to be stuck in the old ways of doing things. Let's face it, any company that intends to make progress need to get to grips with this form of technological prowess. The truth is that your business does not need to be a technology leader to do this. Social Media Marketing can be learned and it needs to be. The impression of an old-fashioned, staid organisation can be a strike against your business (in the minds of potential customers). A social media presence conveys a sense of being open to new things, of being aware of what's going on today. It kind of states that you want potential customers to know about some exciting developments in your company. In addition to these, what you're sharing on social media provides people with an opportunity to take a peek into your business.

It portrays the business as being outward facing

A social media presence naturally shares elements of being outward focused, just by taking this step of exchanging information so freely. An outward-facing organisation is much more attractive than an inward one.

It says that you are interested in what people have to say

Social media platforms are mainly about interaction - public interaction. As long as your social media postings encourage interaction, whenever the interaction happens the potential message customers get, is that you are interested in what matters to them and want to help them. A business that keeps to itself and doesn't make an effort to connect with people send a clear (and entirely different) message through its inaction.

It says effort is being made

Your business says "we're making an effort" when you establish yourself on social media platforms. This action communicates to your clients and prospective clients that you are willing to come and meet them where they are, you value them enough to want to connect with them

.

There are also some additional benefits below:-

- Social media provides you with more exposure to the outside world.
- A positive social media campaign will boost your credibility and can help establish you as an expert in your industry.
- Social media offers you the quickest means or medium for interacting with prospective clients, thus enabling you to give excellent and up-to-speed customer service.

The latter three benefits in particular will ultimately lead to increase in revenue and eventually the exponential growth of your business.

Chapter 4

Advantages of Social Media over Traditional Media

Social media has undergone astronomical growth in the last number of years; it is fast overtaking traditional media such as TV, radio and print. A huge number of companies and organisations are riding on the back of this significant growth; they are using social media as a tool to promote their businesses and connect with customers.

It is now a fundamental aspect of the marketing mix for most businesses. The beauty of Social Media's sharing feature amongst active users is the fact that it enables marketing campaigns to spread at an incredible pace.

Advertising campaigns set up on traditional media are set up once, however, in social media they can be instantly updated which means that if a crisis arises, there can be immediate intervention. This not the case in traditional media, this gives social media another edge over traditional media. However, intervention in a crisis must be done in the right manner to prevent a catastrophe.

Because of all the points about marketing and advertising where traditional and social media differentiates, social media has become more advantageous. Besides, it can easily be said that social media will increase its impact by expanding its user community in the near future. That's why all medium and small-sized enterprises are taking their position on social media platforms and shifting from traditional to social media.

There are a few points below highlighting the differences between social media marketing versus traditional marketing:-

Format

Both Social and Traditional media offers distinct message formats. TV provides one of the broadest visually appealing and creative platforms. Stories can be presented with characters, visuals and movement. It can be either in written or verbal copy; it could also have sound and product demonstrations.

Radio has no optical component, and the message effectiveness is based on creative copy mixed with powerful narrative and sounds. Social media is quite extensive and so ranges from video streaming through to YouTube videos, including brief text copy exchanges as well as marketing on Facebook or Twitter.

Engagement

The development of social media has coincided with a heightened emphasis on customer engagement in advertising. Companies are looking for more direct, real-time and interactive exchanges with clients who will provide instant feedback and personal connections.

On the other hand, TV and radio advertising are known more for churning out passive messages targetted at creating an unforgettable experience that eventually leads to buying activity. Follow-up research is usually needed to ascertain if customers got the message and reacted.

Low cost

One of the most distinct differences between the two media is cost. The costs of using traditional media tend to add up quickly, as you have to design ads, buy air time and space - not to mention billable hours if you use an advertising agency. In contrast, most social media outlets are free to use. Of course, your social media efforts can be outsourced to a marketing or specialty firm for a price, but you will end up saving money if it is done in-house and this can be done well.

Traditional media can prove to be extremely expensive, especially for small businesses. However, most social media is completely free to use and the only cost to businesses is the time staff needs to spend updating profiles and interacting with customers and contacts. Companies can use social media to create and distribute articles, videos, audio and more for a fraction of what it would cost for this content to appear in traditional media.

Access for all

In many ways, social media is accessible to anyone, regardless of the size of their company, its turnover, or their contacts, it, therefore, levels the playing field for businesses. Furthermore, social media tools can be accessed by anyone, whereas access to traditional media can require a significant amount of money and a superb network of media industry contacts.

Simplicity

Traditional media production can require a high level of skills, training and specialist equipment. However, social media channels are extremely simple to use, even for people with basic IT experience. All that is needed basically is a computer/laptop or similar device and internet connection.

Global reach

It's true that traditional media can reach a global audience too, but this is extremely costly in most cases. Through social media, businesses can instantly reach a global audience as quickly as they can reach customers based locally. It's easy to tailor your content for each market segment too.

If you happen to hit the jackpot and produce a piece of content that does go viral as well, there's no limit to the number of people you can reach, at no extra cost – the trick is in hitting that sweet spot that makes content eminently shareable.

Get to know your customers

Social media offers unprecedented opportunities to build relationships with your clients, primarily due to its real-time and participatory nature. Companies can obtain feedback, get their ideas tested and manage customer services efficiently and directly, in a way that they cannot with traditional media.

Traditional media marketing is one-way, but with social media, customers have the opportunity to choose the messages they accept and those they search for. Social media affords an atmosphere of proximity between businesses and their clients which provide opportunities to communicate, rather than simply push out sales messages.

Flexibility

With social media, companies can be extremely flexible and adapt instantly. Information can be updated, altered, added to and commented upon in a way that's impossible in a printed advertisement or article, or a TV or radio ad. Since information can be published in seconds, you can ensure it's always current and up to date.

Measurable

Feedback with social media is immediate, whereas traditional media often needs to be monitored and evaluated over an extended period of time. With social media, businesses can experiment and test marketing messages and approaches, gauge user feedback and tweak the messages accordingly.

Traditional media relies on long-term tools to measure performance and gauge the effectiveness of brand messaging. However, with social media, almost instantaneous measurement can be carried out as customers respond to companies and each other across different platforms. The moment a company notices that the response is negative, they have the chance to course-correct promptly, thereby minimising damages to the business.

There is an ever-growing number of easy-to-use social media measurement tools, many of which are free and provide fascinating and valuable insights for businesses.

No Barrier

There are almost no barriers to creating or distributing content on social media. It can, therefore, be safely said that besides the time you spend creating content on social media and production costs of the content (if it is outsourced), social media marketing is free.

Meanwhile, the three traditional media avenues - TV, Radio and Press have very different costs.

TV is traditionally the most expensive medium regarding cost. Even in local markets, you can spend thousands at a minimum to produce a commercial. Then you would need to spend at least a few more thousands to buy a package of ads for air time on a local TV channel for a month. Radio advertising tends to be a cheaper option for local businesses than TV. Production of the adverts are usually more affordable than TV as well.

Advertising in the Press, however, is the cheapest of the three traditional media.

There are almost no barriers to creating or distributing social media content. Businesses can generate and distribute articles, audios, videos and more for a fraction of what it would cost to advertise the same on traditional media especially, TV which is customarily the most expensive of them all. It can cost thousands of pounds to advertise on TV, radio and newspaper tend to be more affordable, but even then it can still cost hundreds of pounds.

The high cost of advertising on television and radio poses a significant barrier for small businesses with little advertising budgets. Meanwhile, every business regardless of size or turnover can access social media and the benefits of promoting on social media. The primary barrier to access advertising on traditional media is usually cost and that is almost non-existent in social media.

Ease of use

It is relatively very easy to use social media platforms; all it takes is for someone with basic IT skill to have access to a computer and internet connection. It is also quite easy to learn such skills, and there are many readily available platforms to learn from and access to such learning are easy and tend to be free. On the other hand, traditional media can require a certain amount of skill and expertise and require specialised training if the skills need to acquired.

Relationship Building

Social media affords companies the opportunity to build relationships with their customers and audience, mainly because of its real-time and participating nature. Companies have the chance to test ideas, request for feedback and manage customer services directly.
It is not easy to do this on traditional media. With social media, companies can be extremely flexible and adapt instantly. This is mainly because information can be updated, altered, added to and commented upon in a way that is impossible in a printed advertisement or article, a TV or Radio ad. Also since information can be published in seconds, you can ensure it is always current and up to date.

Accurate Targeting

Another key advantage of social media is that it can be used to target audiences far more accurately in terms of isolating exactly who that brand or product wants to advertise to. Moreover, customers have a participatory role as they are always sourcing information and products of interest and distributing them to others.

Agility

Social media has a unique advantage of allowing brands to adapt to customers buying and sharing habits almost immediately. Traditional media requires expensive investments by corporations who are unable to react as swiftly as the market demands.

Newness

The fact that consumers are always preoccupied with whatever is new is barely exclusive to social media. However, social media maintains the gleam of being "new" because it re-engages consumer attention. It can also continually evolve in response to consumer demands.

With traditional media, although the content can change the format of distribution hardly changes and when it does, it is slow.

Interaction

While social media can interact with its target audience, communication in traditional media is unilateral. Traditional media broadcasts the brand's advertisement on channels like television, radio and magazines but it's almost impossible for users to contact the brand.

On the other hand, in social media, the brand shares ads-purposed posts on its social accounts. Thus, on these channels, the users can easily contact the brand with their comments and get feedback from the brand. At that point, we can observe that the brands are also transmitting their questions and comments from traditional channels to social media.

In social media, the brand can set a target audience. In traditional media, the brand's ads appeal to all of the TV audience and magazine readers, except the actual target audience. While the point is a large community in traditional media, in social media, after deciding on the target audience, running the ads and marketing activities only on this audience is more beneficial as a feedback for the brand.

Exponential growth

With social media, there is almost unlimited potential for exponential growth and this is repeatable and can be achieved at a low cost. In order to achieve the same exponential feat on traditional media, a huge amount of money has to be expended. Also, more money has to be paid to have a repeat performance.

Proximity of time and distance

Time and distance have invariably disappeared as an obstacle between consumers and businesses worldwide. As such, social media has created a globally connected world which never existed before. This has provided a tremendous potential for either success or failure dependent on how well businesses understand the dynamics they need to make it work.

Maximum exposure

With social media, businesses can receive a significant amount of exposure. It is much easier to increase brand exposure on social networks because of its accessibility and integrative marketing process.

Building communities

Social media has the added advantage of enabling businesses to build online communities through means such as tagging, using hashtags, and search features. It is easy to identify pertinent partnerships, social influencers, and competitors on social media.

Tracking

Businesses can easily track and monitor social activities on social networking platforms, so this causes conversion ratios to be higher on social media. The fundamental advantage of this is that it is easier for businesses to identify what works well and areas that need improvements regarding their social media strategy and execution.

Intimacy

With traditional media, it is necessary to broadcast to thousands or millions of people at once; this robs it of the specificity and dialogue that can be achieved through social media.

Social media marketing is practically taking over from traditional marketing because of its cost effectiveness and interactivity. Another significant advantage that social media has over traditional media is that campaigns can be sculpted and toned to accommodate a particular target market with almost continuous updates as the market's tastes and interests change and evolve. However, because social media is still more or less at the inception stage, some consumers have a hard time differentiating between traditional versus social media even though they are light years apart.

Differences between Traditional Media and Social Media in a nutshell

Traditional Media

One to many communication
Untargeted mass marketing
Monologue message
Focuses more on branding than communication
Supply-side thinking
Viewing customers as targets
Segmentation
Mainly offline techniques
Aims at mass awareness
Doesn't use many insights or data for decision making

Social Media

One to one or many to many communication
Personalised, mass customisation and targeted
Dialogue
Focuses more on communication than branding
Demand side thinking
Views customers as partners – CRM, feedback
Communities
Predominantly online techniques used
Awareness created through targeting

Uses customer insights and data to help with marketing strategies and decisions

There are some similarities between traditional media and social media and knowing what those similarities could assist you with planning your message and communicating it more adequately.

Although many businesses are getting on board with social media, others are still wary of it and reluctant to make a break away from traditional media. However, with its low cost, immediacy and interactivity, can your company really afford to ignore social media?

If you're intimidated by the world of social media, you can dip your toe in slowly. Get online, listen, get a feel for the different platforms, and start experimenting with content and interaction. You'll soon see how much more social media can offer than traditional media.

Chapter 5

Starting your Social Media Campaign

Of all the means available for you to attract people to your website or blog or to make them know about your business, social media has been shown to be the cheapest, most predictable and controllable of them all.

You must be wondering why; here you go:-

Search Engine Optimisation which has been making waves recently is more of a game of chance than of certainty; this is because you never really know if your site will be at the top of search results given that there are millions of other competing sites on the web.

Word of mouth which is another means, is the most inefficient: since you'll not be able to get to a lot of people with this technique.

But with social media, thousands (if not millions) of your prospective clients are already waiting to hear about your business. With social media, you can tailor your campaign to just the right group of persons that will eventually make a purchase. Finally, social media is extremely efficient; with little effort and resources, you can build a significant social media presence within a short amount of time.

This is beginning to sound good to you right? It sure should!

However, a lot of people out there misunderstand the entire concept of social media marketing. In the following section, the myth of social media marketing will be unravelled and what it is will be disclosed to you.

The Myth about Social Media Marketing

What Many People Do Not Understand About Social Media

The myth of social media marketing is this:-

A lot of individuals are looking for a secret formula that will guarantee social media dominance overnight.

And here is the truth:-

There is no secret formula to apply to ensure your social media success. There is no trick to learning when it comes to social media marketing; it's all about interaction with your audience and clients.

Using social media is all about engendering interaction and consistently compelling people to engage with you and then sharing useful contents and your product or services with them. This is the core of social media marketing, nothing else.

More emphasis on what interaction means will be made.

Many social media enthusiasts are obsessed with the number followers they have and the number of likes that they get on their post; or even more with the amount of traffic that their sites and blogs receive. But this is not the metrics of social media success.

The right metrics of social media success is in interactions - *it is in the number of comments and sharing that you get on your posts and updates*. This is truly how to measure engagement - the more people you have engaging with your content, there becomes a higher likelihood that they will share it. This will eventually cause an increase your online exposure.

How do you encourage or increase interaction on your content?

One sure way to increase interaction is to both encourage your readers to comment on your content and to make sure to take the time to reply their comments. This is what it means to engender interaction and conversation.

The Why of Social Media

The essence of social media campaign is to drive people to your website or blog; it is not to increase your personal popularity, but the popularity of your business and in extension your product and services. This is the WHY of the social media.
Individual social media profiles should be used as outposts to attract people to your website or blog. The focus of your site or blog should not be on sending readers to your outpost. It is crucial that you grasp this fundamental concept.

Creating Your Social Media Profile

So far, we have learned the true meaning of social media marketing and it benefits. In the next chapter, you will be taken through the steps of starting your campaign on the following available social media platforms, they include:-

1. Facebook
2. Twitter
3. LinkedIn
4. Google+
5. YouTube
6. Instagram
7. Pinterest

The process involved in creating an account in each of the above-listed platforms for your business will be covered. Each chapter will take on one platform. This is so as to cover every aspect of the process that is needed. At the end, a section will be given to deal with content creation; the importance of knowing what to post and then there will be information on growing your social media pages and boosting your campaign.

Chapter 6

Establishing your business on Facebook

The following will be covered:-

- Insights about Facebook
- Setting up a Facebook page for your business
- Identifying your audience
- Creating content
- Advertising
- Performance measures, tracking and strategising.

Facebook

Facebook was launched in 2004 by Mark Zuckerberg and his fellow Harvard University friends. Anyone who registers can create a user profile, find their friends and add them. They can exchange messages, upload status updates, photos and videos. Users will also get notifications when their friends update their profiles. Furthermore, users can join groups that they are interested in such as church groups, work groups and so on. Facebook is free and it is an excellent means of communication.

You can promote your business on a Fan page that you set up and also advertise with Facebook Ads, the ads placement service is both easy to use and cost effective.
You can also set up Facebook groups which you can use to connect to all the "friends" of your business who join the group.

Facebook Insights

Facebook, as of the first quarter of 2017 had 1.94 billion monthly active users [1]. Subsequently what this spells out is that if Facebook were a country, it would be the biggest in the world, substantially larger than China which has a population of 1.37 billion people. This is a compelling reason for every business to have a presence on Facebook as part of their marketing strategy.

Setting up your Facebook Page

Note: There is a huge difference between a Facebook page and a Facebook account: while individuals use a Facebook account, Facebook pages are mostly used to grow a business or a brand.

Before jumping right into the steps for setting up a page on Facebook for your business, what are the benefits of doing this, what do you stand to gain from this process?

Below is a list of some of the benefits of getting your business on Facebook.

Creating a Facebook page has the following benefits:-

- Increased discover-ability: Facebook is one of the most used social media sites and one of the most visited websites in the world today. Getting your business on such a site (in the form of a Facebook page in this case) will expose you to the world and let people quickly see your business. It will give you access to an already made and available audience for you to sell your business to.
- Increased efficiency and productivity: Your Facebook page will help you reach out to a large number of people who are signed up to the platform in time and with minimal resources.
- Increased Interaction and connection: Given the inherent and sophisticated interactive nature of the platform, setting up a Facebook page for your business will enable you to interact more with your audience because of the chat and comment features on the platform.
- Analytics and tracking tools: information on your marketing activities are provided via Facebook's insight tool. This will help you with planning and strategising to increase the effectiveness and output of your campaigns with ease.

One very crucial aspect in the process of creating a page for your business is in choosing an address and a name. The address is in this form "facebook.com/yourcompanyname."

Note: *To increase the impact of your Facebook address, make sure to include it on your business cards, your blog, your websites and all other marketing medium or materials.*

When choosing a name for your Facebook page, it is important to choose the name that reflects your company, using the name of your business or company is your best shot.

Have it in mind that your Facebook page is an extension of your business, it provides you with a very easy way to share updates and information with your clients and fans, it also helps you to engage with your customer on a more personal level via private chats and comments.

Okay, enough of beating around the bush let's jump straight to creating a Facebook page.

Steps for creating a business Facebook page

1. Open your browser and enter this address www.facebook.com/pages/create. It will be best to use a desktop or laptop computer.
2. Enter the name you want to use for your page.
3. Enter your preferred address.
4. Choose a category for your page.
5. Use the drop down list provided to select a correct category and provide all the required information.
6. Click on the get started tab and follow the instructions provided on the screen.

And voila! You have your Facebook page ready.

- **Identifying Your Audience**

Having set up your Facebook page, identifying your audience and target clients is the next task on the list. Facebook does not only give you the resources to reach a lot of people, but it also allows you to reach the particular group of individuals that your business targets and this group can be regarding age, sex, religion, occupation, marital status, etc.

After identifying your target audience, your next step is to point out specifically how your business is going to help them; this will be your selling point.

To build your audience and fan base, getting people to like your page is imperative and it can be done in the following manner:

- **By invitation**: that is, using the ‘invite friend button' to invite your friends and family to like your page. This is the way to let people know about your page, encourage them to like your page and even share with their friends. This is the primary audience that will help establish your credibility and spread the word about your business on Facebook.

- **By sharing the page**: like your page and share with your friends, who else will if you do not do it first.

- **Through email**: get a list of emails and regularly send them emails, spreading the word about your new page and reminding them to like and share your page.

As you strive to build your fan base and grow your audience, it is important to note that it is not all about the number of likes that your page has that count. Rather it is about connecting and interacting with even the few that you may have, that counts; they are the ones that will make purchases and further spread the word about your business.

Content Creation:

Your Facebook page is ready and the likes are also coming, it is now time to make business come alive on the page with useful content. It is important to always have your readers at the centre of your content creation - be it an article, photo or video. You should only create content that your readers will find interesting, inspiring and useful. Your content should communicate the essence of your business to your readers and how you are going to help them.

There is no hard and fast rule when it comes to content creation; you have to experiment with different kinds of posts to find out what works best and interests your readers and stick to it and also take note of what is not functioning at all and discard it.

When creating content, a few things are important:-

- Being authentic and original
- Being consistent and regular
- Being responsive to feedbacks and comments

If you are sharing only what you are interested in and excited about, it is most likely that your readers and audience will be excited about what you have created as well. Regularly posting will help you build trust and constantly connect with your audience.

You can schedule your post using online services that provide these service; this will help maximise your time and improve efficiency. It is of the utmost importance that you are responsive when people comment on your updates, ensure that you respond, so your readers are aware that you are listening. You should always keep them up-to-date.

When a particular post receives a lot of engagement, turn it into a successful promotion to reach more people.

Advertising: Using Facebook Ads to Grow Your Fan Base

Now that the readers are available and you have started posting content that both interests and satisfies them, the next step to take is to find other people who are likely to be interested in the product that your business offers. One way to do this is with Facebook Ads. Facebook Ads work very well as a means of getting your products to just the right group or category of people that will make purchases.

Creating Facebook Ads for your business is quite simple. Facebook Ads can be set up from the admin panel on your Facebook page or using the Ad creating tool.

It is essential that you target different categories of audiences with different Ads. You can create different Ads for diverse groups of people that you intend to reach. Readers are more likely to respond to message and updates that directly concerns them or that are tailored to meet their particular need and interests.

Performance Measuring, Tracking and Strategising

Facebook provides a lot of tools to measure the success or failure of your Facebook page activities. One of such tools is the Page insight (this was mentioned earlier in the section about benefits of a Facebook page). Your Facebook page insights show how your page is performing. It reveals which type of content is thriving, the age, gender, occupation and location of people who consistently engage with your content, so that you can concentrate on them, promoting and using them for targeted Ads.

Tracking the performance of your page provides data to plan, strategise and improve your promotion and targeted Ads campaign so as to increase the efficiency of your campaign and subsequently increase the activities on your page.

References

[1] https://www.statista.com/statistics/264810/number-of-monthly-active-facebook-users-worldwide

Chapter 7

Utilising Twitter

Twitter is the next big platform that you can't afford not to utilise. This is a free online social networking service that allows users once registered to send short messages limited to 140-characters called "tweets." A person that is not registered on Twitter can only read tweets but not post them.

Twitter was set up in March 2006 by Jack Dorsey, Evan Williams, Biz Stone and Noah Glass and launched by July 2006. Twitter spread worldwide at an alarming rate, with more than 100 million users by their sixth anniversary in 2012 who were posting 340 million tweets per day.[1] By July 2014, Twitter had grown to have more than 645 million registered active users, with 135,000 users signing up daily them being active users.[2]

You can easily keep your followers up to date with the latest information about your business using Twitter, they communicate with you too and stay Informed. You can also use Twitter to promote your business or specific events and raise awareness about such events and for generally creating a buzz.

Twitter users are inclined to be more engaged and more pro-active when using their accounts, so it is easy to reach them through tweets and retweets. You can also advertise your business and events using the Twitter advertising platform to reach a wider audience. Twitter is also a very useful to monitor real-time conversations about what people are saying about your business. This will enable your marketing and management teams to see what people are actually saying about your company.

You can turn your tweets into real-time testimonials - Your tweets should be used as marketing tools. For instance, a coffee shop displayed happy tweets from their customers on a flat-screen TV in the store so everyone could read them.

Twitter Insights

As of the first quarter of 2017, there were 328 million active monthly users on Twitter [3]. There are "500 million tweets per day and around 200 billion tweets per year" [4]. A significant number of Twitter users (over 80%) use mobile devices to do their tweets and followings.

Given the above stats, it is evident that your business has to be on Twitter to tap into the enormous possibilities it presents and to reach out to more people. This will consequently increase your online presence and sales.

Creating a Twitter handle for your business is quite easy and straightforward, it involves the following steps:

1. Go to www.twitter.com on your browser. You can use your computer or mobile device.
2. Click sign up or create a new account.
3. Provide the information required and that is all.
   Voila! Your Twitter handle is ready for use. In creating your Twitter handle one important aspect is in choosing a username for your handle. As stated in the previous chapter about the steps in creating a Facebook page, using the name of your business or company as the username for your handle is your best shot on this platform as well.

If you do not create a handle for your business on time and claim your name on the platform, others might end up using the name before you, which could become a major issue for your brand and your readers who might be confused concerning who you really are. The increased popularity of Twitter has led to a market where handles can be bought and sold. It is thus imperative that you sign your business up on Twitter immediately to reserve the handle for your company and also any business that you intend to start in the future. This will ensure that your brand is uniform across all social media channels.

A word on Branding

No one will ever want to follow an account or handle which does not look legit or one that looks fishy. Thus before you commence any active engagement on Twitter for your business, some things must be put in place and these are essential to register the credibility and uniqueness of your brand.

The first thing is to fill out your user profile completely.

Second is your bio: look over your website, blog and all other profiles you have online and draft your Twitter bio from them, this will help people find you and easily recognise you on Twitter. Truthfulness is needed here.

Next is your Twitter background image. Using a background that is uniform with the design (colour, format and logo) of your company is the best option. The background provides an opportunity to include information like contact details, pointers to your website or blog or information about your products and service which are not available on your profile.

The avatar of the account should have the company's logo.

The Road to Becoming an Expert

Despite its character count restriction, Twitter is another form of blogging, though a much shorter version (micro or mini blogging). The rules to succeeding in blogging and managing a website therefore also applies, regularly tweeting about your business and expertise will increase your online presence and reputation in that field; people will start to follow you and look out for your updates as answers to their question in that area.

Note: <u>www.twitterfeed.com</u> *can be used to synchronise your blog post with Twitter so that your updates are posted on Twitter automatically immediately they appear on your website or blog.*

Besides providing regular post and tweets on the field that your business covers, another way to grow your reputation on Twitter as an expert is to have Q&A sessions with your followers. Here you can answer all the questions that your audience have about your business or product which you have not clarified in your posts and updates.

These two paths, always posting and providing answers to questions are the sure ways to establishing yourself as an authority on Twitter. This will subsequently lead to increasing your online presence, growing your business and increasing profit.

Designing a market plan to boost your Twitter followings

Twitter marketing plan elements include the following:

- **Email Signature**: Chances are that you have already placed your website or blog URL as well as contact information details as part of your signature when signing emails.You now need to add your Twitter handle as well. This is a free way to promote your Twitter account with every email that you send.
- **Website and Blog Home Page:** You can use your website (if you currently have one) as a platform to promote your Twitter handle to people who are interested in your products.
- **Presentations:** Your Twitter handle can be included on the last page of any presentation that you give with a call to action for your audience to follow you on Twitter.
- **Business Cards**: You can add your Twitter account to your business cards.
- **Networking through Twitter**: Always using the tagging symbol when communicating, commenting or retweeting on Twitter will get you more responses and more followers as it gives whoever reads it the opportunity to follow the link to your handle.

The above suggestions when followed or applied is sure to improve/grow your Twitter following.

Note: *The same rule applies to any social media network, the more followers that you get on Twitter, the easier it will be to grow your community. And as mentioned earlier, content is king, so you will have to provide your followers with quality tweets and updates* consistently.

Despite the fact that more social media platforms are springing up, Twitter is here to stay. The user base of Twitter is ever increasing; more people are signing up and using the platform to communicate on a daily basis. This is an efficient medium to grow your business; get your brand on Twitter and begin to experience an increase in reputation, sales and profit.

References

[1] https://www.statista.com/statistics/282087/number-of-monthly-active-twitter-users/
[2] http://www.internetlivestats.com/twitter-statistics/
[3] https://blog.twitter.com/2012/twitter-turns-six
[4] http://www.statisticbrain.com/twitter-statistics

Chapter 8

Linking Up on LinkedIn

When it comes to the list of professional social networks, LinkedIn is number one. Linkedin, according to wikipedia is "a business- and employment-oriented social networking service that operates via websites and mobile apps". [1] It is mainly used by businesses and professionals.

Launched in May 2003, LinkedIn has gone through a lot of design and functionality improvement and changes, however, it still has its primary purpose intact - which is connecting professionals.

Linkedin Statistics

Some stats will help to comprehend the usefulness and effectiveness of LinkedIn fully. As of the "third quarter of 2016 LinkedIn had 467 million members up from 450 million members in the preceding quarter". [2] This means that the user base of LinkedIn continually grows, which only implies that LinkedIn is not a website to overlook when attempting to establish your social media authority.

When it comes to hiring skills, finding supplies for your business, generating leads and increasing the awareness of your brand, LinkedIn is a powerful network to utilise.

Kicking off on LinkedIn

To register on LinkedIn, follow these steps:
1. Visit www.linkedin.com
2. Fill in the required fields such as name, job title, company, etc.

Once you have completed creating your account, the next step is to work on your profile page where you can add more details to your account about who you are and what you do.

It is imperative that you add as many details as possible to your profile. Your photo, name and headline are the three most important items that will show up on LinkedIn.

When it comes to professional matters, the first impression is paramount. It is, therefore, important to place a lot of focus on the photo you use for your profile. This is because it is what people will look at first, so make sure it is very clear and professional; do not make the mistake of leaving it blank as this may send some signal of non-authenticity to anyone viewing your profile.

When selecting your profile name, it is important to use the name that you are known as professionally. Sometimes, it is also wise to use the name that you are known by, e.g. if your name is Timothy but everyone knows you as Tim, then using Tim will be advisable.

Also, your headline needs to be very descriptive and highly informative, it should contain information about your current work location and positions. Furthermore, make sure to give a detailed list of your skills and their corresponding expertise on your profile. It is important to make all your contact information up-to-date this includes your username, phone number, email address. Your handles and accounts on other social media platforms can also be added. Your contact details are of extreme importance for the effectiveness of your profile.

On your summary

Now it's time to tell your story in the summary section. This story includes who you are, your life goals, your passions and career goals. The summary provides you with the opportunity to reveal a little bit about yourself and your personality.

After including all the information required in the above-listed points, it is important to walk through your profile meticulously to ensure that it has been completed, if not add more details as may be needed. Ensure you utilise every single field or opportunity available to mention your skills, expertise and experience. Talk about yourself and your business, use the opportunity to sell yourself to the world and prospective clients.

Creating Connections:

This is the most crucial aspect of LinkedIn. It is where you actually connect to people on the platform who are interested (or will be interested) in your brand or products. The more connections you have on Linkedin, the more often your profile will show up in Google's search results. This might tempt a lot of people to connect to just anyone that they come across; however, connection on LinkedIn should be approached in the same way as networking in real life is done, i.e. you should connect with people that you know or people who are in your line of business.

The above-stated points are essential; they are to be taken seriously and followed to the letter if your LinkedIn campaign is to succeed. Like every other social media platform, LinkedIn will help you find new prospective clients and thus increase your sales.

References

[1] https://en.wikipedia.org/wiki/LinkedIn
[2]https://www.statista.com/statistics/274050/quarterly-numbers-of-linkedin-members/

Chapter 9

Google+ Authority

Today, it is almost impossible to do anything on the internet without a Google account or Google product sign up of some sort. Google+ is Google's social media product. It is a relatively newcomer to the game of social media networks, but given the vastness and extreme, innovative approach of the company, signing up on Google+ is paramount.

In this chapter, you will be walked through setting up a Google+ account and the chapter will end with a note on the uniqueness of Google+ over other social media platforms.

Signing up on Google+

This is the first thing to do to use any of Google's product. To use Google+ you will need a Google account, if you already have one, simply skip this part and go on to the next - on setting up your Google+ account. If you do not have one, creating a Google account is quite easy. Just visit www.google.com and click on sign up or create an account. Enter the required fields which will include your name, domain (i.e. name@gmail.com) and some other information to verify the account. Once you are done with this, simply sign in and then click on the button located on the left side bar or type this link http://plus.google.com.

Creating a Google account will give you access not only to Google+ but to a lot of Google products which includes Gmail, Calendar, Docs, YouTube, etc.

Making Progress on Google+

Now that you have a Google account, let's start working on our Google+ profile. When you join, a public Google+ account will be automatically created for you. It is important to use your real name (that is your actual name) when you sign up in order not to violate the terms of service and engagement.

Next, is creating your profile. Your gender and a profile photo will be required. When you are creating a business profile or trying to establish an authority online, it is important to choose a quality photo of yourself or your brand. Using the same photo across all your social media outlets makes it very easy for your prospective clients to recognise you.

Then you start adding people to your circles. Google+ usually provides a lot of suggestions on this page. If you have another email account, you can import your contacts from that account or simply search through Google+ for people using their names or even their email address.

Working on Your Profile.

Now it's time to add more information to your Google+ profile. This will involve where you work, academic and residential information. As it applies to all other social media profiles, the more details you provide on your profile, the easier it will be for people to find and connect with you. Google+ also introduced the concept of circles thus allowing you to control who sees certain contents or information and who does not, based on the circles that they are added to. So you can create business circles to post information about your business and contents for your subscribers whilst keeping personal information private.

Creating Pages on Google+

In addition to your personal page, Google+ allows you to create additional pages to promote your business. On the side bar, click on the more icon to start creating pages on your Google+ account. Provide the information required such as the name of your page, the category, and a brief description of your page. To boost traffic to your site, include your website address. You will also need a photo for this page, using your business logo or your headshot is the best thing to do, you can also provide a custom background picture different from the default provided by Google.

After providing all the necessary information, you can preview your page to see it the way other people who visit your page will see it. This is very handy as it gives you the chance to see your profile through other people's eyes and make necessary adjustments if need be.

Creating and Adding Content

Just like in every other social media outlet, you will have to provide compelling and useful content on your page consistently. Your contents can be photos, videos, articles and links to other useful resources that will be of interest to your clients. You can promote your page to your circle of friends as well as link the page to your website or blog.

The Uniqueness of Google+

One of the major unique aspects of Google+ which make it different from Facebook and other social media platforms is Hangouts. Hangouts allow you to connect with your readers and clients through video. You can create a Q&A section on your page where your readers can ask questions, about your brand and you provide them with answers. This significantly increases customer satisfaction, as well as your social media presence and reputation. Additionally, it will help you grow your brand and ultimately increase your sales and profit.

Google+ will be around for a for a long time (at least for as long as Google remains the king of web service providers), the platform is ever growing and ever evolving. More businesses are using Google+ to increase customer satisfaction and improve their online exposure. The steps needed to get your business running on Google+ and enjoying its enormous benefits have been stated in this chapter, go ahead and get your business on Google+.

Chapter 10

Boost Your Social Media Authority with YouTube

YouTube is a video-sharing website with headquarters in San Bruno, California. It was created by three former Paypal employees – Chad Hurley, Steve Chen and Jawed Karim, in February 2005. Google bought the site in November 2006 for US$1.65 billion; YouTube now operates as one of Google's subsidiaries. [1]

“As of July 2015, more than 400 hours of video content were uploaded to YouTube every minute and according to YouTube CEO Susan Wojcicki, more than 1 billion hours of content are consumed on the platform every single day as of March 2017”. [2] A lot of online business owners have made the mistake of striking YouTube off their list of social media outlets. But the fact is that YouTube as at the time of writing this book is the third largest social media site on our planet taking up to 20% of all social media activities. It is therefore almost insane (seeing the above stats) to ignore YouTube when you are trying to establish social media authority in your niche or industry.

YouTube has obviously grown exponentially over the last ten years. It boasts been the highest trafficked site on the internet. This makes it obvious to see why Google fought to buy it. The videos that can be found on YouTube varies from funny videos, documentaries to sports highlights and musical videos to helpful tips, name it and you can find it on YouTube.

YouTube is the "go to" website to get your 60 seconds of fame and has people fighting nail and tooth to get the most views. However, before jumping off to start publishing your videos on YouTube, there are a few things that you have to put in place. The following sections will cover these important things after which we will jump straight to publishing your video on YouTube at the end of this chapter.

Benefits

YouTube videos are excellent tools for capturing the attention of people; your business can easily get worldwide exposure if a video you upload goes viral. YouTube videos can be shared easily online on other social media platforms such as Facebook, Twitter, Instagram and other similar platforms.

YouTube has high traffic volumes so publishing videos on such a huge platform gives your business the potential to access a great deal of publicity

Google owns YouTube so YouTube videos are ranked highly on Google's search pages regularly. Google also rates videos as being important so this contributes to the high ranking status they give them.

Defining Your Purpose

What is your purpose for creating videos for your business? There is one question you have to ask yourself. This will save you a lot of energy and resources since you will only be focussed on creating a particular category of videos with simpler messages to portray your purpose and goal. With videos that are well crafted with targeted messages, you are more likely to get higher returns in the form of increased fan base and ultimately sales.

To decide your purpose, you need to ascertain what you intend to achieve with your videos and hence determine the metrics with which to measure the level or extent of your video campaign success. These metrics might include:

- Creating sales
- Generating leads
- Increasing brand awareness
- Introducing/advertising new products and services
- Enlightening the market and your clients
- Providing a level of pleasure or entertainment for your clients

Once the purpose for your video campaign is set and your metrics of performance is decided, your next task is to determine the class of audience that you want to reach. This will ascertain the content of the video and its presentation.

Types of Video

The next thing is to determine/decide the category of videos that you want to create for your YouTube campaign. These might include any of the following types of video:

- Animation videos
- Presentation videos
- Interview videos
- Illustration/Whiteboard videos
- Montage videos
- Time lapse videos
- Talking heads videos
- Case study videos
- On-location videos
- Product demo videos
- Documentary videos

Once you have decided on the type of video, the nature of the video must also be chosen. The various tones of video include:

- Informal
- Formal
- Colloquial
- Technical
- Irreverent
- Traditional
- Competitive
- Collaborative
- Creative or
- Corporate tone

Your purpose and goal will help you select which tone to use for your video.

You also have to make sure that your video matches your brand. It should buttress your corporate image and goal, telling more about your business and your product.

A word on length of the Video

This is one of the most important parameters to consider when creating your video. As much as this is important, it is tough to tell what length is best. However, speaking in general, videos that are two to five minutes in length works best in terms of audience engagement.

Research from surveys indicates that videos between 90 to 120 seconds have the highest views. However, the length of a video is determined by the purpose and aim of creating the video, so there is no hard and fast rule to the length of your video; though short is always the best.

To throw some more light on this concept of video length, its purpose alone should determine the length. For instance, there is no way you can provide enough information about a subject such as leadership in a minute or a minute and a half; you may, therefore, have to consider a longer length of say, 10 to 20 minutes for this. If on the other hand you are creating a video to entertain or humour your audience, a one-minute video will be ideal, a product presentation or demonstration can be done in 90 seconds and so on. It all depends on the purpose of the video and nothing else; the use determines its length.

Your videos should match your existing brand and content.

Uploading Your Videos

When you have made the decision about the purpose and perfect length of your video, you've created it and it's all ready for publishing to your readers, well done! However, there are still a few more simple steps needed to get your video on the web and they are highlighted below:-

Getting Your Video on YouTube

The first step you need to take is to set up a YouTube account using the Google account you created earlier, (if you do not have a Google account, go back to the chapter on Google+ and follow the steps outlined there to create one). It is important that you use the name that you want to be known as, which invariably should be the name of your business or brand. After this is done, sign in into your YouTube account and click on the upload button at the top of the page. Select the video that you want to upload (this should obviously be saved on your computer or tablet), choose the privacy settings her the video (that is the circle of people you want to see the videos) and then publish.

Further settings include editing basic info, video settings and choosing between notifying and not notifying your followers of your new video.

Just like it takes time to succeed in anything, establishing your presence on YouTube does take some time. You need to consistently upload interesting and engaging videos for your existing audience and also to reach out and attract prospective clients and customers.

YouTube is a sure way to create visual content about your brand, spreading the word regarding your product and improving your social media presence. It provides you with the resources to reach your customers with visual and well-detailed content about your product, thus further educating and enlightening them. This will, in turn, improve your online reputation, customer satisfaction, fan base and ultimately sales.

References

[1] https://en.wikipedia.org/wiki/YouTube
[2] https://www.statista.com/topics/2019/youtube/

Chapter 11

Using Pinterest

The saying that a picture is worth a thousand words also applies to social media marketing and social media platforms like Instagram and Pinterest are here to help you tell your story with graphics.

Pinterest and Instagram are great ways to promote your business and improve your social media authority through images and pictures (and even videos on Instagram).
As of October 2016, Pinterest had 150 million monthly active users worldwide. [1]

Benefits of using Pinterest

Pinterest help increase the visibility of your business as you pin relevant and worthy information on the platform. People are able to repin and share those photos, this enhances visibility.

Your audience can get a feel of what your business is like by looking at the images and videos you upload, this can get them to tip over and make the crucial decision to come and do business with you, either by going to your website or by coming physically to your building.

It is easy to connect to your audience and build relationships on this platform as you can draw people in and engage your audience with your postings.

Creating an Account on Pinterest for Your Business

To create a Pinterest account for your business, enter this URL into your browser www.pinterest.com/business/create On this page, you will be prompted to enter your name, business name and business category or type including your website. As stated in the preceding chapters, it is important to use your business name as your name on Pinterest.

The selling point for your Pinterest account is the "about" section so make sure you take care in crafting a quality "about" section in just 160 characters. The "about" section tells your followers the purpose of your business and what they stand to gain from your page.

To further increase traffic among your other social media accounts, ensure you link all your other social media accounts to your Pinterest accounts (you should also do same on all other social media platform, i.e. link all your social media platforms together). Make sure to add your website URL to your Pinterest page. It is usually verified and when done, it will appear more prominently on your page, encouraging people to click on it and also gives you the ability to use the analytical tools available on Pinterest.

Adding a profile picture is also vital. This image should represent your brand so that your followers will be able to recognise your page easily. Using your business logo is the best option.

Finally, the next step is to create your boards.

For your boards to stand out, it is imperative to provide them with unique names, (preferably short names of 2-4 words), a cover photo or image and a pin for each of the boards.

References

[1] https://www.statista.com/topics/1267/pinterest

Chapter 12

Setting up your business on Instagram

Instagram was launched in October 2010. Registered users are allowed to upload photos or videos to the service. They can add their locations through geotags and “hashtag” their posts, “hashtagging” will link their photos to other content on Instagram with the same subject. Users are also able to connect their Instagram accounts to other social media platforms, which enables them to automatically share the photos on those platforms as well.
Instagram amassed popularity very quickly, it had one million registered users within its first two months and then 10 million within a year. Instagram announced in April 2017 that the number of registered users had gone up to 700 million. [1]

Benefits of using Instagram

Your business can use Instagram to engage its audience as Instagram users tend to be more engaging than users of other social media platforms. It is easy to build a sense of community and trust amongst your audience with Instagram as you can easily emotionally connect with people using photos and videos uploaded on this platform. Instagram is an effective platform to establish relationships with your audience this could include existing customers and potential customers.

Getting up and running on Instagram is simple. The steps needed to give you a heads up are listed below:-

1. Install Instagram on your mobile device by downloading the app (using the app store or play store for android).
2. Sign up for an account. Using the name/username that you used for your Twitter handle is the best strategy in order to keep brand consistency.
3. Next, is adding a profile picture. Using the same image that you used

for your Twitter handle is also the best option. Connect your Instagram account to your other social media accounts; this will notify your followers of your new account on Instagram.
After setting up your account, the next big step is creating content for your Instagram followers, and this is where a lot of businesses struggle or get it all wrong. When creating content for your Instagram page, it is crucial that your images come in a mixture of fun elements combined with content on your business. Stories appeal a lot to readers so try telling a story using images.

Apart from photos, videos can also now be posted on Instagram. However, care should be taken in ensuring that the length of the videos used on Instagram are not as long as those posted on YouTube.
When creating your Instagram page, it is important to create a unique visual sense. Focus on what engages and interests your readers.

References

[1] https://www.statista.com/statistics/657823/number-of-daily-active-instagram-users

Chapter 13

Increasing Fan Base and Interactions

Hopefully, the fact that you have gotten to this chapter means that you have successfully set up accounts for your business on all the major social media platforms/sites.The next item on the agenda is to learn the steps that need to be taken to attract more followers to your social media pages and boost engagement on these pages. A lot of people try to accomplish this via daily routines, like having a set number of updates every day and posting on those pages. Though important, it is not the key thing to do to promote engagement and get more followers.

Social media is more about engaging with your readers and followers to improve satisfaction and grow long-lasting customers. This is also a means to gather data and feedback needed to keep your product up-to-date.

Below is a list of things you can do to gain more followers and boost engagement on your site.

- **Adding featured stories to the timeline of your company on Facebook**: Stories have a way of appealing to the minds and senses of people. The more stories about your business posted on your timeline, the more interest and engagement it will generate, so much more than simple or standard posts will.

- **Encourage likes with incentives**: Encourage people to like your page and posts on Facebook and other social media pages by promising them (and fulfilling the promise) gifts, discounts or free products.

- **Do not flog a particular Ad to death**: if there is one thing that will both annoy and discourage your readers from following you, is when they see one Ad coming up over and over again. Rotate your Ads, make sure that you create different Ads that can be rotated on a regular basis.

- **Let your brand logo or image be known**: One easy way to create a consistent brand image for your business is to use your image on all social media platform timelines and updates.

- **Regularly listen and respond to your readers**: Show your readers that you are constantly listening to what they have to say. Always ensure that you respond to all the comments that are left on your updates and posts as promptly as possible. This will demonstrate the fact that you exist and also that you hold your readers in high esteem. In addition to this, you can host a question and answer session, so you will get to know the concerns of your readers and attend to their needs either by improving your products or customer care services.

- **Use insights regularly and discover users' active times**: Apps such as Tweriod (the name alone tells you that it is for Twitter) will let you see your users most active periods of the day. Also, Facebook page insight can give you similar information for your pages. You can use such information to organise and schedule your updates and tweets, so it fits in with your readers.

- **Increase your reach by following new people daily on Twitter, Instagram, etc.**

- **Organise a followers lists**: Putting your followers into different lists is an efficient way to send out unique messages to each group. Thus improving targeted outreach, maximising resources and increasing the effectiveness of your campaign.

- **Landing page customisation**: Each of your social media accounts should lead to a landing page on your website or blog. This landing page can provide discounts, gifts and offers to the customers for visiting your site via your social media page. This is the most efficient way to get followers to sign up to your mailing list.

- **Hangouts**: This comes in handy on Google+. Make sure to participate in hangouts that are organised by others in your business line; this will help you connect and engage with others. You can also organise hangouts to give your followers access to your expertise and experience in the industry.

- **Recommendation of contents**: share the content that is recommended regularly on your social media pages on your profile. Sharing quality and unique content with your followers is a great way to increase credibility and engage with them.

- **Hangouts on Air**: This has to do with videos. You can stream your Hangouts on Google+ to your followers on YouTube at the same time. These does not only keep all your followers up-to-date, but it also is a quick and easy way to get videos on YouTube.

- **Commenting on the content of others**: Apart from sharing contents with your followers, you should also comment on the contents of others. On Twitter, you can use your hashtag to direct people who read your comments to your page.

- **Closely Monitoring your activities:** This will help you know what is working for your audience and what is not+. This is the most important aspect of social media marketing. You have to closely monitor the activities on your social media accounts, know what to change, improve or eliminate. Study the behaviour of your readers, their location, time of activities, etc. Not doing this is not using social media for your business at all.

These are a few steps you can take to increase participation and the effectiveness of your social media campaign. As has been stated earlier, getting people to know about your business and products is all about interaction. Treat your social media outlets like actual networking events; start conversations with people, talk a lot about your brand and product and watch your business grow.

Chapter 14

Social Media Profile Maintenance

A lot of people after having their social media profiles/pages up and running, think that is all it takes and therefore neglect them. This is sometimes done unknowingly, due to focus on creating content, posting, tweeting, uploading videos, etc. On the contrary, in order to maintain a positive image on the social network, maintenance is required. You have to ensure that your social media profile and information are regularly reviewed and are up-to-date at every point in time.

Keeping your social media profile up-to-date is highly important, below is a list of things that you can do to ensure that your profiles are maintained and highly effective.

Keep a check on image size requirement:

Your images play an important role regarding making your first impression. Make sure that you always check the size requirement for each page and always keep your images within that specification.

Social Share Button:

Be sure to provide sharing buttons for as many social media platforms as possible or available. There is no way of knowing the preference of your customers for content sharing, thus making all the buttons available for your readers will give them the opportunity to share according to their preference: if a client likes to share on Facebook, retweet, pin it on Pinterest, etc., they can do so easily.

SEO

Keywords are certainly not a thing of the past; no matter what you have been hearing. You might be interested in learning that social profiles are included in search engine results, this means that your profile is a huge selling point for search engine optimisation. Your profile should thus contain a lot of keywords related to your industry. You can use keyword tools to get important keywords associated with your industry.

Get Reviews From Readers

Social media is essentially about engaging your customers in interactions about your business or products. To further this, encourage your clients to leave reviews about their experiences with your services or products, either on your social media page or website/blog.

Comprehensive Description of Event or Promotion

If you are organising any event or any promo, make sure to provide enough information about the event, so that readers will know when they have to register or sign up (if that is required for the event), and how they should go about it. Do not leave your readers in the dark concerning your events. Many users may click on the 'I am going button' and may not have any clue on how they actually have to go about it.

Using Hashtags

You can use hashtags (words or phrases preceded by the # symbol) to make your content stand out. You can use it to promote an event, product promo, video or update, etc. Hashtags should always be descriptive to keep your followers interested.

Make Your Customers Feel Recognised

As your fan base grows and your social network community begins to expand, some of your followers or customers may start to feel not useful or appreciated anymore. They may want to neglect your brand or product entirely; One sure thing to do to ensure that this does not happen, is always to use their names when you are responding to their questions, comments or feedbacks.

Title and Meta Tags

Your business name has to be included in the title tag and meta description of your blog or website. Not including it might create a lot of difficulty for people who are looking to find you. It is important to use your exact business name, not a word close to it or anything but your company name; no matter how catchy the word may seem to be.

Adding your business name to your meta description and title tags will make it easy for your readers who are searching for you to find you quickly.

Important note:

If you are just starting out on social media marketing, it is important to focus on just one social media outlet at a time and when it appears that you have done a great job on that one, you move to the next social media outlet. By rule of thumb or general view, Facebook is typically the first to start with, as it is the easiest to understand, set up and use. Then when you are done with Facebook, move on to the next outlet, making sure that the information and content provided in all of these social media platforms are coherent and support one another.

Your basic information and profiles should be complete and updated regularly, including a clear and easy to understand description of your business, your logo and URLs. These can be scheduled to be done every month, every week or in any other manner as deemed fit and convenient for you.

Chapter 15

Scheduling and Social Media Automation

You will start to realise that it takes a lot of time to keep all your social media pages up-to-date with relevant content and information. This can sometimes be discouraging, but not to worry, there is a great social media tool called Hootsuite to the rescue.

Social media management tools such as Hootsuite provide services that give you the ability to schedule posts on your Facebook page and Twitter. It helps you monitor your conversation and much more. Visit Hootsuite (www.hootsuite.com); this can save you a lot of time and energy that would otherwise be required to update your social media profiles manually.

However, with social media automation software and system utilisation, it is important not to go to the extreme of total automation and abandonment of your social media platforms.

The question now is how do you automate your social media pages but still remain in touch with your readers and audience?

The answer is to practice automation correctly; do not start and end your social media campaigns in automation. Automate what has to be automated and stay engaged consistently with your readers. Remember social media marketing is all about engagement and interaction, once this is missing, everything is a waste of time.

Social media should not be treated like an oven where all you do is set it up and forget about it. Rather, the treatment you dish out to your social media presence should as though you were baking cookies. You know that your job is not over when you put the cookies in the oven, you've got to prepare the next set. You also need to constantly check on the progress of the ones in the oven to ensure that they are being baked the right way. If you want the cookies to turn out right, you do not stop until all the cookies are done and out of the oven.

Working Both Hard and Smart

Automation aims at making your job more efficient. It can help you take your daily work hours to merely a few minutes, thus giving you the opportunity to spend time on more pressing matters thus saving you a lot of time.

Automating Social Media Campaigns

To properly automate your social media campaigns, the following steps should be taken.

Knowing when to automate and when to engage with your readers:

With social media automation systems like Hootsuite, it is quite easy to become addicted when you start using it. However, it is necessary for the sake of your business that you resist this temptation. Some things are meant for automation and some are definitely not. It is imperative that you know what is what, in order to avoid potential social media crisis.

An excellent rule of thumb that you need to follow when it comes to sharing content is the 5-3-2 rule. It can be explained as follows:

* Content from others should contribute to five of your posts, however, they should be of relevance to your audience.

* You have to be responsible for writing three of the posts.

* The last two posts should be personal and unrelated to work. This is the 5-3-2 rule.

You have to focus on your audience when you maintain a schedule like this and it will enable you to be on top of your marketing plans.

Social media posts that are not urgent can be automated. This includes automating your RSS feed as well. This process will allow you to share your posts across many outlets at the same time. Checking the formatting of each site is important in setting up this process so that the output will be uniform with that of the site's requirement.

What Automation Tool to Use?

Hootsuite is a great resource and works with many of the top social media platforms including YouTube, Tumblr, WordPress and Instagram.

The program can easily be set up within your website which means you can automatically share your content across all social media platforms.

You can also set up releases in any manner that you want by choosing the content that gets shared as well as the timing of your posts. Everything that you want posted can be placed in a queue, properly sorted and published when they are scheduled to be published, thereby making this tool extremely beneficial for your social media marketing.

Creating the Ideal Posting Schedule

Next, is to create an ideal posting schedule. Hootsuite allows you to put all of your information on a queue, which means you can specify the time of the day when a particular post is to be published. This can be done for the entire day and even a week.

In creating your schedule, always endeavor to get your content to your audience at a prime time during the day. Based on your audience, it might be in the morning, lunchtime, evening or even at night. If you want your posts published at some exact times then, the following are some criteria to watch out for:-

- The time you will be available to respond to comments (remember, social media marketing is all about interaction).
- The time when your posts are most likely clicked, shared or commented on.
- The time zone of your fans.

You can use your Facebook page insight to get information on the above-listed criteria. For Twitter, you can use tools such as Tweriod to analyse your followers, in order to tell when most of them are active on social media.

As a rule of thumb, when it comes to determining the time of the day when most people are active online, here are some stats to guide you:

- Twitter engagement is 17% higher on the weekends.
- Twitter users are 181% more inclined to be on Twitter during their evening and morning commutes.
- The maximum number of retweets occurs around 5 pm.

Concerning scheduling posts for when you will be available online to interact and communicate with readers - this depends on you. Schedule your posts for times when you will be available to respond to the questions and comments of your audience; as this is the whole essence of social media marketing - communication and interaction.

Staying Involved

As mentioned and emphasised throughout this book, social media is all about interaction. Even if you are setting up automation, it is still important that you stay online and are involved in the entire lifecycle of your updates.

This might be difficult to do, but using online tools can make it easy for you to pull through. One way to stay in touch and involved is to use Google Alerts. This service provides you with email updates anytime there is any activity on your content e.g. when you receive a mention. You can then give the necessary or appropriate response.

Most importantly, set aside a time every day or at the very least a few times every week to visit all your social media profiles and engage with your audience. You do not have to follow an exact prescription, merely use any timing that will fit into your schedule.

A Note on Content

In social media marketing, content (of any form: articles, photos or videos) is critical! In getting to know the right content for your target audience or readers, it is important to try new things all the time. Once you determine what posts are gaining a lot of interaction and engagement, you can repeat them and concentrate on producing more of such posts. The key is always to be experimenting and noting the things that work best and eliminating those that are not functioning.

It all comes down to personal communication and knowledge of your readers. Reading all sorts of information about what has worked for others and copying everything to the letter is not the best action to take. This is simply because audiences vary from blog to blog and from one social media platform to another. Content that works for one person may not work for another person and vice versa. This is due to variance in readers and audience.

No matter the number of articles you read about engaging your readers, it will be ineffective compared to the effectiveness of doing what you believe is right for your audience. It is imperative that you measure what you do, how impactful it is and then adjust your techniques accordingly. This will increase impact and help grow your business.

Chapter 16

Key Thoughts on Social Media

Truth be told, the fact is social media is here to stay and if you are going to set up any type of business presence online, then you must be established on each of the main social media sites mentioned in the book.

To get started, you may have to choose a favourite social media site (Facebook is an excellent choice as it is easy to use and set up) and create your page there. Once you have it running smoothly, you can then go to the next social media site of your choice.

Most people will typically start with Facebook or Twitter as these are two of the largest sites. While it is important to become established on both of these sites, it is also critical not to forget about the other social media sites such as Pinterest, Instagram, Google+, etc.

Google+ is kind of a newcomer to the social media game, but it is gaining much ground as a lot of people are joining the platform on a daily basis.

LinkedIn is the one place to meet professionals in your field or industry.

Instagram and Pinterest provide great outlets for photos and videos.

Though overlooked by a lot of people, YouTube is a major player in the social media marketing game; not only is YouTube the third largest social media site, it is also the second biggest search engine. If you want to be successful, ensure that you establish your business on YouTube.

Spending some time on each of your social media pages will help you to build your authority for your niche within a short period, which can lead to higher profits for your business.

Chapter 17

Online Marketing and Advertisement

Letting the world know about your business

Taking a critical look at traditional advertising like the use of Yellow Pages, the Newspapers or TV commercials, some common features or characteristics will be found in these mediums of advertisements or platforms. Firstly, they are expensive and there is no real way to measure their effectiveness or return on investment.

We will analyse these traditional means of advertisement one after the other.

First taking a look at the use of Yellow Pages, do you know where your Yellow Pages book is right now? That is, if you have one.

The sure answer to that question for most people is a big NO. However, if you do have a copy of the Yellow Pages and perchance know where it is.... When was the last time you looked for a business in it?

The correct answer most likely would be that it was a long time ago.

Unfortunately, many businesses still spend thousands each year on Yellow Pages Ads. Studies have clearly shown that the average person who uses Yellow Pages is over 70 years of age. Now if that age group is not your target market, then you definitely have to apply a new method to your marketing strategy.

TV Commercials and Newspaper Ads are obviously used to tell people all about your products or services with the hope that they either need it when they see your advertisement or hopefully remember your Advert when they require your service.

As for Newspaper Ads, the question is - do you get the local paper on a daily basis?

The likely answer, which will most probably be correct is No. This is in line with the fact that 24 out of the top 25 Newspaper companies are recording a decline in sales of Newspapers.

Newspaper companies aim to keep their readership and to do this, they place the reader's interest first, thus putting articles in prime locations thereby dumping your Ads in whatever space that is left off from the published articles. This implies that potential clients can't tell where to look to find information about businesses even if they wanted to use the Newspapers as a source of such information.

As for TV Commercials, not only is it almost impossible to measure effectiveness, nowadays, most people watch recorded shows and most times skip the commercials altogether. This simply makes placing Ads on such a platform a waste of time and resources as the return on investment is minimal.

Life Saver – How the internet saved the day

The Internet and mobile device platforms have revolutionised the world of marketing and most businesses are just starting to become aware of this with only a small percent of early adopters existing. All the credits to high-speed wireless networks, mobile devices, communications software, and social platforms. Marketing is now being transformed to a largely all-digital discipline for local businesses.

The internet is quickly replacing old-fashioned advertising methods listed earlier such as newspaper ads, printed business directories like the Yellow Pages, direct mail coupons, the radio and TV ads. Your business doesn't have to sell products or services over the internet before you can use the internet to market it; online marketing is effective for every type of business.

Local consumers increased usage of the Internet and mobile device is gradually driving all businesses to learn how to reap the benefits of using these new platforms to make their products and services known to prospective clients. Even more so now that the internet is interactive, consumers are sharing their experiences with local businesses - both positive and negative- thus helping companies to use these feedback and reviews to better their customer satisfaction and improve their products.

Taking a look at some stats: - Google has over 3.5 billion searches every day, which totals about 108 billion searches monthly(using a 30-day month), over 28 billion a month(or 27% of all searches) are local. This simply means that a lot of people are actually putting in their geographical location to their search queries.

An example will explain this better:-

Say for instance you are in Camden Town in London and you are looking for an Optician. For your search to be easier and more efficient, the chances are that you do not just type in 'Optician' into the search bar. Instead, you will include your area like 'Optician in Camden Town.' The tendency is usually to add the location to narrow down the search to your closest proximity. After all, how useful will a search result be if you cannot benefit from it because the distance makes it impossible to access the service? People are looking to acquire products and services right where they are.

Here's another fascinating statistic: 82% of local searches are followed up by an action: - visit the store, a telephone call, an email or better still, a purchase. So when people are searching locally, it means they're ready to take action and more likely to make purchases of the products or services they are inquiring about. These people are the so-called purchase-ready or purchase-driven customers.

Chapter 18

How to capitalise on the internet to grow your business

Local Internet marketing is based on helping local business owners put information about their companies and products online so people can easily find them at the exact time that they're looking for them. What is good to learn is that there are a number of ways that businesses can put information online so that local people can find them when searching. Real time relevance and satisfaction is what makes the internet's approach to advertisement different from every other form of advertisement.

The Internet uses a technological approach and highly sophisticated tools to find the most relevant information about businesses and nearly everyone uses it. Now, old fashioned methods don't even produce enough results to even pay for themselves anymore. Alternatively, local internet marketing provides a strategy for local businesses to put their information in a lot of places so that people can find the information at the exact time that they need the products or services.

Rather than spend a huge amount of money on ineffective means of advertisement, business owners can now see a lot of value for the money expended on using the internet local marketing strategy.

Getting your business online via a website

Starting off your internet marketing campaign

To get the best out of internet marketing, you will need a great website. In fact, a robust site can actually be the key to the beginning of your internet marketing campaign. This will help you generate highly targeted customers.

In addition to getting a robust and functional website for your company or product, you have to know what your target audience wants; this is the only way you can provide potential customers with content that will be interesting to them. As the manner of the internet is, you will be selling your business ideas to visitors who are seeking the type of service that you have to offer and are ready to make purchases. Your content should be informative, easy to read and should speak much of your products and brand.

Educate your visitors. Give your audience something they can use. Rather than merely copying the same information that is on other websites, make sure your content is unique. Tell people who visit your site something that will be relevant and meaningful. This is what will keep them coming back time after time.

Another aspect is to create desire. A well-built website should give web visitors the desire to want to know more. Keep the content engaging and unique. Include any new information relevant to services offered by your company.

Email marketing is a great resource for attracting prospective customers to your site. While the website is the starting point for your internet marketing strategy, your mailing list will entice people to visit your site.

It is vital that you know your market and what your customers will need or will be requesting. Your website should be focussed on your target market. Consider who is most likely to visit your site. One important question to ask yourself is - what will they want to know? When you understand your market and know who your clients are, knowing what to tell them will be easier.

When creating content for your site, always use examples or scenarios. It is essential that you give your web visitors something they can relate to in a very distinct way. If you end up writing something that describes that person, you will find that you would have won or gained that customer for yourself. This person might end up buying your products later.

Your content enables you to create the needed interest that will draw your prospects closer. Not all your prospects will be in the same situation, therefore, include different scenarios. In fact, it is highly likely that you will have a diverse audience. Using different case studies or adding a lot of different scenarios will appeal to a large range of readers or potential customers.

It is paramount that the information on your site is clear. Your readers should have no problem understanding your information. Use a language that is at the intellectual level of your readers.

Always remember to explain industry vocabularies when used and should only be used when it is required. Explain things clearly, so that they easy to comprehend. You want your customers to relate to you on a very personal level. Easy to grasp content will draw a lot of readers to you, make them stay and thus increase your sales.

Chapter 19

Turning clicks to cash

It can be deduced that one of the primary goals of most businesses is to make a profit. It is, therefore, vital that those who visit your site convert to clients. The key to a successful website is conversion.

Below are steps to implement on a website aimed at conversion i.e. turning clicks and visits to cash.

- **Provision of quality content about products/ services offered:-**

Ensure that the information provided is clear and concise. What will appeal to web visitors, especially those who are conducting an initial search, is information that is easy to understand.

You need to capture your visitors' attention immediately. You, therefore, need to put the most crucial information first. Consider the most important points you want visitors to know about and ensure that these are published before anything else.

- **Set up a website that is easy to navigate:** -

Website layouts that are confusing or difficult to follow content will cause visitors to exit your site and go elsewhere for the needed information. Write all content with your potential readers or clients in mind. Be explicit about what you can do for them and how helpful your services or products will be. Highlight the benefits of your services or products and tell them why they should choose your business.

- **Design your website specifically for your target audience:-**

This invariably means that you create each page with different kinds of visitors in mind. For instance, you might link a particular page to a specific Ad; that page could include information about the services you provide. So, when a visitor is searching explicitly for this type of information, it is readily available to these potential clients so that they can reach it with ease and speed.

This will eliminate the task of navigating the entire site just to find the information they want. This might not always be the case; on the other hand, another visitor might be reading an article about your products and services and follow a link to your home page. This particular individual is not looking for a specific type of info, but rather is looking for something in general. It's all about directing your readers or visitors to the right place that will satisfy their particular needs.

- **Always use an active voice in your content to keep visitors motivated:-**

Your content should be engaging and make your readers want to continue reading. This is dynamic and appeals a great deal to your audience and often your web visitors feel as if you are speaking to them directly. It helps create a rapport, which can quickly end up in a conversion.

- **Increase the trust between your business and your visitors:-**

Trust is the foundation of every good relationship and it will serve you immensely when it comes to promoting your business. You want your prospective clients to believe in you and feel confident about the products or services you provide.

Your business will benefit hugely from well-thought-out web pages designed with your target market in mind. An effective website usually begins with a successful online marketing plan. The above tips will help you build and grow a site that will help you grow your business.

Chapter 20

The value of a website to your business

To harness the immense potential of the internet and apply it to your business, the number one, or the most important tool that you must have is a great website. Your website is where relevant information about your business, products and services will be located and it is your direct link to potential prospects.

What are the benefits of having a website?
Below are but a few ways a site will be beneficial to your business:

- **Benefit #1**

Customers want a particular place where they can go to get information, if you fail to establish your internet presence, your competition will beat you to it. Your site can make you stand out from the rest. It should depict who your business is. Tell readers about the products or services you provide and the various means of contacting you. Your website must be informative, easy to read and navigate.

- **Benefit #2**

An excellent website helps build trust. It informs web visitors that you have something important to offer and gives them a place to go where they can learn more. This affords you the opportunity to establish your online image. It also shows your expertise in the field.

- **Benefit #3**

A great website increases the chances of others learning about your business. The internet is currently the number one source of information for almost everyone, most especially in the area of search engine utilisation. For this, search engine optimisation (SEO) is crucial. The ultimate goal is to receive high ranking on your web pages. Your website will become more visible online the higher the individual pages on your site rank. The content of your site should include keywords potential customers will use to find you. A well-optimised site will place you high in the rankings.

- **Benefit #4**

In addition to wanting to keep the content of your site easy to read and navigate, all your pages should be catchy. Many businesses choose a particular theme for their websites, which helps give it a uniform look throughout.

It is imperative to choose a theme that is relevant to what you have to offer. Put usability into consideration while ensuring the content and all elements will capture the attention of your web visitors. A website that is well-designed, easy to navigate and which contains useful information tends to bring the visitors back.

- **Benefit #5**

Your website is your source or point of the first impression. This is especially important to those web visitors who are hearing about you for the first time online. Your web pages must look professional; they should be user-friendly and provide your potential customers with every information they will need to begin taking advantage of your services or acquiring your products.

Always incorporate up-to-date information; this is essential. A website that is not updated in a long time will gradually lose trust until users completely abandon it. You should keep your site active with real content and up-to-date information. Add some useful articles or blog posts. This will show that you visit the site frequently and are in touch with the needs of your readers or clients.

Make sure all contact information is correct. Visitors who are unable to make contact to make inquiries definitely will go elsewhere. You can avoid this by providing several ways in which they may get in touch such as a contact section, a feedback mail, a discussion section, etc. Think of your website as a part of your overall business and allow it to grow. If you give your website the right attention, it is bound to serve you well.

The importance of an excellent web copy

A lot of web users (including you) often do not make it very far down a search result page before trying a new search. Most people can't be bothered to look through hundreds of search results and simply don't do it. It is, therefore, crucial to have a high website ranking as a consequence of this reason. Because this is the only way, you will be visited by readers via the search result pages. Presenting information the right way is one of the ways of getting high search engines rankings. It is also critical to get several pages on your website to rank high. This places you at the top or near the top which will result in your name and URL being seen multiple times and users will often click on a name they see repeatedly.

A great website copy clearly informs the users of what to do i.e. it presents a call to action. For instance, you could incorporate a page on your site listing the benefits your products or services provide. This ought to be done in such a manner that web visitors will be prompted to contact you with a desire to learn more. Once the benefits are listed very clearly on your page, they would be easy to understand. The same is true concerning whatever other actions you want them to take on your website.

You also want your visitors to feel something when they go to your site. A great website copy does this by evoking emotion. Many web visitors may not be familiar with exactly what products or services you provide but, upon finding out, they ought to feel a particular emotion. Perhaps it is hope or maybe even excitement because they have finally found the information they need. It doesn't matter what it is, you have made a difference. It is therefore not only about what you say, but it is also about how you say it.

Ideally, your web copy should tell compelling stories. These could be in the form of testimonials. People often respond well after hearing about the experiences of others. You could even add some information about the reason you started the business and tell your web visitors about your expertise in that field. The pages of your website should tell stories in such manner that it speaks directly to your visitors. This is arguably one of the simplest ways to turn a potential client into a converted customer. This is also an excellent means of gaining trust. Prospects will want to come to you if they feel you know what you are doing and will satisfy their needs.

Your online credibility will be established to a large extent by your web copy. You must write content that will inform, convince, identify with your visitors and inspire a particular action that needs to be taken. One of the consequences of this is the sharing of information because a visitor who becomes a customer may go on to recommend others to visit your website and invariably, your business. Your online presence should lead to the expansion of your business. It can help you reach people who aren't in proximity to you, but who might greatly benefit from the products or services you have to offer.

Chapter 21

Getting traffic to your website

In this section, seven major strategies for creating a dominating local online presence have been listed. When these devised tactics are properly executed, it can result in new customers coming to your local business. The strategies can also help you build and grow an effective and commanding online presence.

Search Engine Optimisation - Securing Your Page Ranking

As the name implies, Search Engine Optimisation (SEO) makes a website more visible to search engines. The primary ways to optimise a website are through the following:-

Firstly, creating great content.

Secondly, using specific keywords that people search for on a consistent basis.

Thirdly, interaction on your website from people visiting.

Fourthly, having other sites pointing to your website - this is called back linking.

When Google or one of the other search engine crawls (looks at) a site and sees that other reputable websites (referred to as authority sites) have links pointing to your site, the relevance of your site increases and thus moves your site higher in the search ranking.

The other important key is to have links on your site that point out to other high-ranking authority sites such as CNN, YouTube, etc. What happens is that when the search engines notice that your website is pointing to some high ranking sites with great information, it benefits your site as this helps to move your site up in the search result rankings.

The other part of SEO is using keywords. The question to ask yourself is - what are the words that people are searching for when looking for your products or services? It really doesn't matter much what you want to show up for because people may not be looking for that. It is, therefore, critical to get this right. People must be looking for your products or services and these are what your keywords should be.

This is not as difficult as you may think when it comes to local marketing. A personal business survey or analysis can be carried out in your local environment. For example, as a person in the medical field, you may ask a number of individuals what they type into the search bar when looking for a particular medical product or service. The result from this survey could provide enough data on the keywords that you should include on your website.

Also to make the task easy, there are a lot of tools out there that can supply you with keywords in your industry. There are keyword tools available on a few search engines that can give you valuable information such as how many searches people are actually doing and how strong the competition is.

As much as keywords help bring your website to the top, Google is now friendlier to original content than purchased traffic. Before, the majority of site rankings were based on technical attributes. Things like on-page SEO, overuse of keywords (keyword stuffing), backlinks, etc. (which indeed really helped websites to rank high) but now Content is King! The search engines use an ever-changing algorithm to decide what is displayed on the first page. These days, search engines rank originality of quality content and visitor interaction (time on site) more than the number of backlinks a website has and rewards accordingly.

Keyword Survey

Keywords are the foundation of SEO. Keywords are the exact terms potential customers are using to find what they are searching for. In keywords, some terminologies such as "long tail keyword phrase" show up. Single keywords are usually too broad as a search term for local searches. Often "long tail keyword phrases" which consists of three to five words together are known are more powerful for local searches because they usually include a geographical location identifier. These are often used for very specific searches and have a higher rate of conversions.

Thus optimising your website with long tail keywords is vital. By placing four to six long tail keywords in your site's code and in the page titles can help your site's ranking. The phrase "social media marketing" is an example of a single keyword while "Social Media Marketing Camden Town" would be an example of a long tail keyword. As you can see, a person searching for the single keyword is looking for general information on social media marketing. On the other hand, someone searching for the long tail keyword phrase is specifically looking results for social media marketing in the Camden Town area.

When creating content for Facebook, Twitter, Blogs, YouTube, etc. always use your keywords in the title first. Content with relevant keywords will help your website's organic ranking, while also having it in mind to avoid overstuffing. This is the excessive use of keywords and search engines do not take this lightly.

Using Google's free keyword tool is an excellent way to find out the best keywords to use for your website or content. You can use it to research particular keywords and it will offer suggestions for keyword phrases that are relevant to your search terms. Google keyword planner tool will also display how many searches each phrase gets per month. This can help you identify the best ones to use so that a lot of people will see your information.

Besides, it will also show you which keywords are rated low, medium and those that are highly competitive. This is critical information because you can work out which keywords to try and rank for. It is often easier to rank for the low to medium competition keywords.

Pay Per Click With Google Adwords

This forms the centre of Google's revenue; Google does adverts by placing your Ads in search results.

You are charged each time someone clicks on your Ad. When web users do click on your Ad, they are taken to the web page you want them to see; this will lead them to some engagement and finally making a purchase from you.

If we use a company dealing in hospital equipment, as an example, they want their Ads to show up in front of web users actively searching for information about "hospital supplies." We can't really tell what web users are looking for exactly, but we know very well that what they are looking for is under the umbrella of hospital equipment and accessories.

The Ads show up at the top of the results page and along the right-hand side of the page similar to Facebook Ads. These Ads are placed above organic search results; they are the ones that people see first. Thus they are the links that get clicked. The reality is that placing your Ads on Google AdWords is likely to yield results.

When someone gets the result for searching "Hospital Supplies" they have the option of clicking on the links that most appeal to them. There is no guarantee that your Ad will get clicked, you've got to have a great headline and body content that intrigues and attracts your prospective customers who might eventually click the link and might end up making a purchase.

Do you want to set up an effective AdWords campaign? Follow these success guaranteed steps:-

- **Setting clear goals**

What do you want to achieve with your AdWords campaign? Do you want a specific number of leads per month? Are you looking to increase newsletter sign ups, increase traffic or generate sales on your website?

Getting Your Facts Right

The following are research points to work on:-

Keywords Research – Use keyword tools like Market Samurai or Google's Keyword Planner to find the most relevant keywords related to your products or services that people are typing into the search engines to find your products/services/ company.

Know Your Competition – You will want to spend some time looking at the competition to see who is consistently ranking at or near the top of the rankings (spy tools like Keyword Spy Tool can be used for this). Pay attention to their Ads and offers. Visit their websites. Sign up to their mailing lists. Purchase their products, know all that is possible about your competition, this will help you strategise new techniques to hit the market with.

Know Your Audience – Where are potential customers buying and reviewing similar products or services online?
Have a look at the reviews being posted. What do those customers love/hate about the competition? What are their needs and desires?

When you answer these questions in addition to your research on your competition, you will know exactly what to do to satisfy your customers and get to the top of the ranking.

- **Landing Page/Offer**

An irresistible offer on your landing page is the absolute key to your AdWords campaign. From your research on your competition, make your offer just a little bit unique/different/better than theirs. It is incredible what a minor improvement over the competition can make!

- **Use Exact Match Keywords**

When initially starting out with AdWords, you should ensure that your keywords list is very limited (5 – 10 keywords) and focused (they must be words that potential customers who are prepared to make purchases are highly likely to be typing into Google). Add all these keywords to your campaign as Exact Match Keywords (this means that your Ads will only be shown when someone types those exact terms into Google). When you do this, your Ads will only appear for searches that are most relevant and not for variations which Google assume are relevant, but aren't.

Over time, you can eliminate the keywords that aren't getting clicks/conversions and expand on the ones that are working and bringing results.

For instance, if "London Oncologist" is working for you, add more Exact Match variations of it to the list, that is by combining the word "Oncologist" with postcodes, nearby cities, and by using variations like "oncologist near London," "best Oncologist in London," etc.

- **Use Unique and Proven Ads**

The Ads should be highly relevant to the keywords they appear for (this includes the exact terms where possible). Ensure that you distinguish your business from the competition by making use of different offers, benefits, etc. Your landing page/offer also needs to reflect the same purpose as your Ads this will help potential customers feel they are in the right place. (If your landing page is not consistent with your Ad copy, it may alter/mar your conversions).

- **Have your Ads tested.**

In order to do this, you place at least two Ads in each Ad group and split test them. The rule of thumb is that you delete the lower performing Ad after each Ad has had least 30 clicks. The Ad should then be replaced by a new one and you should test the new one as well, this should go on until you find the ones that rally work.

- **Track Your Results**

Whatever the goals of your campaign may be, make sure you track your results.

Track your sales, downloads, newsletter signups, etc. with AdWords conversion tracking. You can also use a call tracking service to track phone calls.

- **Collect the Data**

You have the opportunity to obtain data from AdWords that you are unable to get anywhere else. It is of the utmost importance that you take advantage of that.

You can use the keyword data to find keywords that are perfect for Search Engine Optimisation (SEO) for your website.

It is imperative that you test different messages, headlines and offers in your ads. When you find ones that people readily respond to, test them on your landing pages and in other marketing media.

Using Local Online Directories
Your Business Right in Your Prospects Pockets

Local directories are web properties that allow companies to list the details of their business at no cost. These directories can be of utmost important for local businesses. These listings can show up in the online search results and on mobile apps on sites like CitySearch, TripAdvisor, Yelp, Google Maps and many more.

The reason this is crucial for any local business is because, according to a ComScore-Localeze survey, 50% of Local Searches carried out on mobile devices are done using these Directory Apps. What this means invariably is that every potential customer walking around with a smartphone has access to 15 different phone books, these are at their disposal at any second. These people are, therefore, within your reach if your business is listed on these sites.

The next question will be: “On which of these directories should your business be listed in?”

The simple answer is all of them!

Google+ Local it is the largest local directory on the Internet. It actually gives information about local businesses as listings on Google. This allows your website to show up on the first page of Google whenever someone searches for that niche and city. Using our initial example, if you enter "London Optician" it will show up with Opticians in London that can be located on a map shown on Google.

It can be inferred that Google+ Local is a very smart way for any local business to put information online and have it appear on the first page. As a matter of fact, there are a number of businesses without websites that have first page Google listings simply because they have entered the correct information on their Google+ page. This is the power of local business directory.

Compared to Facebook and other popular social media sites, a lot of business owners are not that familiar with Google+. However, with approximately 375 million active users, the site is fast gaining popularity and should be considered as part of your marketing plan.

The creation of circles is one very distinct part of Google+. Friends, businesses, work colleagues, and customers can be included in these circles. The beauty of this is that you decide what you want to share with the people in different circles. You can share specific information with specified circles.

This system enables you to set up business related content as well as content for customers which you can then choose to share in the respective circle. This is an excellent way for companies to use Google+ to tailor their marketing plan for their target market.

An additional benefit of Google+ is that it allows businesses to announce new products, share coupons, host contests, share blog posts and publicise any current promotions. This is an excellent method for companies to share information that is relevant to their customers and assist them in attracting potential clients. Google+ pages also provide companies the opportunity to humanise their business. This can be done by sharing videos or stories about employees and what they do each day.

In addition to the advantages mentioned earlier, another significant benefit of making use of Google+ is that it can positively affect your online visibility. When people interact with your Google+ page, it demonstrates to Google that web visitors are interested in whatever your business has to offer. What Google then does after taking notice is that they will start to reward your activity on Google+ with higher search engine rankings. In essence, this means that when the products or services that you offer are being searched for, you will be found easily as your business will be positioned amongst the top search results that are provided.

Another way that being active on Google+ can be beneficial to your business is that when your posts are properly optimised, Google will take notice. To ensure that your posts are properly optimised, you should include keywords and topics that relate to your particular niche. When optimising the content you post, it is imperative that you incorporate these terms into your content naturally. Adding too many keywords, or including them in such a way that they do not flow organically, may have an adverse effect, as Google does not like that. For you to get the attention of Google, you have to keep your content natural and organic.

Google+ is an invaluable marketing tool for any company. If you are already using social media as part of your marketing plan, you should definitely consider what Google+ has to offer. It is an excellent way to increase awareness about your business and attract new clients.

Getting Google+ Reviews for Your Business

One vital part of your internet marketing campaign is a Google+ listing. But another very invaluable tool that plays a great role in your internet marketing is customer reviews.

The fact is that customer reviews can either make or break you; these reviews are often what provide potential customers the information they use to make a decision about whether to become your clients or not. It is in your interest to acquire a lot of positive reviews; this will enable you to make the most of your Google+ listing.

The question is - How do you deal with this aspect of your Google+ listing?

A number of tips have been listed below to help you get started; these tips will not only show you how to get reviews but also how to respond to them.

- Request for positive reviews.

- This is relatively straightforward. Once you have satisfied customers, encourage them to visit your Google+ listing and write reviews stating their experience. Explain how easy it is to do this and how it will be of benefit to you; if you truly satisfied them, they will be willing to leave a comment on the good job that you have done. Make sure you adequately describe the steps that they have to follow to leave their reviews.

- Google+ provides you with a personalised link that is exclusively for your company. You can send it to your customers' emails and/or regular postal mails for the prime purpose of directing people to your listing. When doing this, be sure to ask directly for positive reviews. Also, this link should be added to all of your company's correspondence including Ads and marketing materials. This is an additional method of promoting your link and requesting reviews.

- Generate a QR code linked to your listing. Place it on everything business related that your clients are likely to see. Add a simple request for them to post positive reviews after visiting your listing. QR codes will take people accessing the internet via smartphones directly to your Google+ listing by scanning. This process is easy and efficient.

- List your company in directories like Bing, YellowPages, Yahoo and Yelp. All reviews submitted to those sites will be automatically linked to and will show up on your Google+ listing as well as your business listings on other directories.

- The importance of receiving reviews cannot be over-emphasised, however, responding to reviews is just as important. Feedback is extremely vital and it can go both ways. Ensure that you always provide a polite response to both positive and negative reviews or comments. It is also paramount that you respond promptly, even if the feedback is negative. This will reassure the negative reviewers that you are paying attention to what they have to say. You should also endeavour to resolve any existing issues through your responses. Express your viewpoint in a manner that is not self-justifying, defensive or insulting.

- For as long as you provide quality products and/or services you will, of course, receive numerous positive reviews. You, however, have to make a conscious effort to thank your satisfied customers for their support and apologise to whoever is dissatisfied or disappointed. You might also offer public referral rewards and coupons to customers through the Google+ listing forum. This will encourage potential customers to give your business a try.

Another compelling aspect of Local Directories are citations created by people leaving reviews of their experience with your business. Obviously, the higher your ratings and reviews, the higher the probability of new customers or clients checking you out. Understanding the effect reviews have on your purchasing decision on Amazon will give you a better understanding of the impact of reviews on your products and brand.

Chapter 22

Mobile Marketing

This is the newest form of marketing. The fact is that you have a mobile phone or most probably a smartphone (and so does a great percentage of everyone out there). The use of mobile phones coupled with internet connection gives people access to a whole world of information at the tip of their fingers.

The Mobile Revolution

It is a well-known fact that the world has gone mobile and that mobile usage has grown at an incredible proportion.

Some companies are now waking up to the fact that they don't just need a great website for people on their computers but also a mobile version of the website for those using mobile devices.

The big question is: - your customers are mobile, are you?

People are using a number of different means such as laptops, tablets, watches, gaming devices and mobile devices. Different devices are gradually becoming more popular means of accessing websites. It is therefore extremely important that your company's website is mobile optimised otherwise you will lose potential visitors.

Even if most of your customers still use desktops and not smartphones to access your website, you should still go ahead to have a mobile-friendly website for your visitors. This is because according to Google "61 percent of internet users are unlikely to return to a website that isn't optimized for mobile browsing". [1]

According to StatCounter figures from February 2015, the number of global Internet traffic coming from mobile devices has increased to 30.38%.[2]

What is a mobile website?

PC Mag has defined a mobile website as "a Web site designed for the small screens of smartphones. Queries to a Web site include the type of browser being used, and when a request from a mobile browser is made, the site redirects it to its mobile counterpart (if there is one) for a more convenient surfing experience". [3]

In essence, a mobile website is a mobile version of your normal website; it is streamlined and designed for ease of use and quick navigation. When a mobile website is in place it means a special code has been placed on the back end of your main website and it will automatically detect how someone has logged on to your website and sends them through to the appropriate place.

It also means that someone on a desktop will see your main website and at the same time someone else on a mobile device will be directed to the mobile version. The mobile website can be designed in such a way that when visitors click on the telephone number while viewing the mobile website, it will call your business directly.

The need to set up a mobile website

A mobile website has to be set up. If you look at a regular website on any iPhone or Android, you will notice that the site is jumbled up. This is usually to do with issues regarding resolution. A regular website was meant for desktop computers and not tailored for mobile devices unless it has been mobile optimised.

On the other hand, mobile sites are well structured and the pages designed to fit the display of mobile devices. This increases the user experience and makes them want to visit your site constantly with their mobile devices. Given the stats that mobile local searches lead to purchase in less than 24 hours, having a mobile site will drastically grow your business, increase readership and increase sales.

A mobile site typically cuts your website down to about four or five pages of the most relevant information that potential customers need to see. That way, when someone goes to that website, they're able to navigate it very quickly. For instance, a site built for a restaurant and designed for mobile devices would have pages such as contact page, menu page, directions page and perhaps a specials page, this way people can get to just the information that they're looking for.

The Mobile Business

Is your website responsive to mobile users? Have you checked to make sure that it is?

Go ahead. Carry out an exercise right now - bring out your mobile device and log onto your website.

Do you have to pinch and zoom to read what is on your website? What do your images and content look like? Do they scale and reorganise themselves? If they do not then your website needs updating as it is not responsive. A mobile responsive website will provide your users a much more positive and less frustrating experience. Moreover you will not lose them as research shows that "61% of people said that they'd quickly move onto another site if they didn't find what they were looking for right away on a mobile site. The bottom line: Without a mobile-friendly site you'll be driving users to your competition". [4]

Test your website

There are a few websites below where you can test your website's responsiveness:-

https://www.google.co.uk/webmasters/tools/mobile-friendly/
http://responsivedesignchecker.com/
http://www.browserstack.com/responsive
http://responsivedesignchecker.com/h

Why your website must be mobile

Some companies are now becoming cognisant of the importance of not just having a great website for people on their computers but also a mobile version of the website for those using mobile devices.

There are a number of reasons why it is imperative that a company invests in a mobile version of their website.

The facts

Google carried out a study about mobile websites, this was conducted by an independent market research firm called Sterling Research and SmithGeiger and some of the results are as follows [5]:-

- "Nearly 75% of users prefer a mobile-friendly site".
- After visiting a mobile website "74% of people say they're more likely to return to that site in the future."
- As much as "50% of people said that even if they like a business, they will use them less often if the website isn't mobile-friendly."
- "48% of users say they feel frustrated and annoyed when they get to a site that's not mobile-friendly."
- "36% said they felt like they've wasted their time by visiting those sites"
- "52% of users said that a bad mobile experience made them less likely to engage with a company."
- "48% said that if a site didn't work well on their smartphones, it made them feel like the company didn't care about their business."

If anything should compel your company to be mobile optimised, it should be the results of Google's study.

Compelling reasons to have a mobile website Google ranking signal:

Google made an announcement in April 2015 that has made it imperative that websites be mobile friendly - “starting April 21, we will be expanding our use of mobile-friendliness as a ranking signal”.[6]

The impact of this is that websites that are mobile friendly will be given higher ranking than those that are not.

The crucial factor to bear in mind is that if your competitors have mobile friendly websites and you don’t, you will be at a disadvantage. This essentially is a "penalty" in effect although it is not called one.

Top search engine results: In actual fact, the search engines now take into consideration whether or not your website is mobile optimised when deciding which websites to display on the search engine results when someone searches using a mobile device. The probability of your website showing up on first page Google is higher if you have a mobile website and someone searches on their mobile device for the keywords for your products or services than if you do not.

More purchases:

Survey has shown that local searches made from mobile phones lead to purchases of sought after products at an average of 24 hours from the time of doing the search; this is in comparison to the number of days or weeks it takes for purchases to be secured from local searches made from computers. As mentioned earlier, in the language of marketing, such customers are known as purchase-driven clients.

Increased numbers of people using smartphones: According to Bloomberg “global smartphone use would have reached 2 billion by 2015.”[7]

"31 percent of mobile Internet users mostly go online using cell phones" (Pew 2012) [8]

"94% of smartphone owners look for local information on their phone" [9]

If you do not have a mobile friendly site already, now may be a great time to make the change and position yourself for 21st century search trends!

SMS/Text Messaging

Another way to utilise mobile marketing is with SMS or text messages. With text marketing, you have to first of all collect and organise the phone numbers of your targeted clients and then market your products to them via SMS.

Why is mobile messaging advertising so important?

The following stats will help explain its importance:-
According to research only about 36% of emails get opened, compared to over 92% of text messages or mobile messages which get both opened, read and responded to in minutes or seconds of being received.

Using a Mobile App to Showcase Your Company

An app can be built just for your company. Many local businesses in this digital age are taking advantage of having apps created solely for their businesses. A mobile app is a software application specially developed to be used on mobile devices such as smartphones or tablets rather than a desktops or laptops. A hub for applications is the Google play store and the Apple store.

The primary benefit of having a mobile app for your business is that it affords your clients the opportunity having your company information loaded directly on their smartphones. This makes it easy for customers and potential customers alike to interact with your business and get access to needed information.

Having an app built for your site and getting your readers to install them on their mobile device is of invaluable benefit to your business.

Below are some of the benefits of building an application for your business:-

- Build customer loyalty - Make your customers feel special by offering discounts, coupons, and promotions just for using your app.
- Instant communication - Deliver instant messages to your customers' mobile phones whenever you wish. While only 4% to 10% of emails get opened, direct messages sent via customised apps are read 97% of the time.
- Create viral buzz - Let customers quickly tell all of their friends about your app via the Social media share buttons which include Facebook, Twitter, LinkedIn, SMS, Email, etc.
- Grow mailing and contact list - Gather names and email addresses directly from your app (i.e. requesting them when they install your application on their mobile devices) and easily export them to a mailing system of your choice.
- Promote special events - Provide up-to-date information about all of your business events, sales, and promotions with an app events calendar that anyone can access.
- Increased Credibility - Having an app designed for your business adds serious credibility to your business, placing a sense of formality of your business in the minds of your readers.
- Keep customers informed - Fill your app with information about your business, service offerings, product samples, menus and more.
- Connect with ease - Make it simple for customers to reach you using one touch calling, email, a website link and also provide direction to your business in your app.

- Get instant feedback - Allow customers to leave feedback about your products and services quickly and share photos. The above list exhausts to a large degree the immense benefits of having an app designed for your business.

Below is a brief stat that will reveal more reasons why you should get an app for your business:-

MORE MOBILE STATS:-

- 50% of consumers use their smartphones to find local businesses.

- Mobile Phones are used more than PC's

- Over 50% of consumers use their phones in stores for buying decisions.

- According to Statistica, the number of smartphone users was forecasted to "grow from 2.1 billion in 2016 to around 2.5 billion in 2019"[10]

- Over 70% of online retailers are now developing a mobile strategy.

  The smartphone market is presently bigger than the PC market and it is still growing.

References

[1] http://googlemobileads.blogspot.co.uk/2012/09/mobile-friendly-sites- turn-visitors.html

[2] http://gs.statcounter.com/#desktop+mobile-comparison-ww-monthly-201403-201502-bar

[3] http://www.pcmag.com/encyclopedia/term/60020/mobile-web-site

[4] http://googlemobileads.blogspot.co.uk/2012/09/mobile-friendly-sites- turn-visitors.html

[5] http://googlemobileads.blogspot.co.uk/2012/09/mobile-friendly-sites- turn-visitors.html

[6] http://googlewebmastercentral.blogspot.co.uk/2015/02/finding-more- mobile-friendly-search.html

[7] http://www.bloomberg.com/news/articles/2012-10-17/smartphones- in-use-surpass-1-billion-will-double-by-2015

[8] http://www.pewinternet.org/2012/06/26/cell-internet-use-2012/

[9] https://www.thinkwithgoogle.com/research-studies/our-mobile-planet-united-states.html

[10] https://www.statista.com/statistics/330695/number-of-smartphone-users-worldwide/

Chapter 23

Blogging for business

Blogs are sometimes overlooked as a significant source of online buzz in comparison to social networking sites, yet consumer interest in blogs keeps growing. Blogs had previously not been taken seriously by a lot of people mainly because they mistook blogs for sites focused only on gossip, politics, sports, etc. Suffice to say that locally focused blogs are powerful marketing tools for smart business owners. The power of the blog comes from the focus on the local community.

Benefits

Blogging on a regular consistent basis helps your business to build trust online as you are able to establish yourself as trustworthy after posting quality content consistently for a period of time.

Blogging enables you to build a community online as your audience is able to respond to and make comments on your posts. You are therefore able to interact with your audience and engage them.

Search engines especially Google loves fresh content, so constant blogging provides those search engines with new content to index, this will inevitably lead to increased visibility on search engine results pages (SERPS).

A blog is also a good platform for reaching out to others. Valuable and interesting blog posts attract readers who are able to give you constructive feedback on your site and send you personal messages through your contact page.

Blogs are very easy to create using one of the popular sites like Wordpress or Blogger. With the use of proper keyword placements, the blog posts can easily rank on the first page of search engines. Be cautious about overloading your posts with too many keywords as Google penalises this action by not ranking high websites that do this. You should also ensure that your content provides value to the audience you are trying to attract.

Make it a habit of consistently posting a variety of content that will captivate your audience, that they find them so interesting that they keep coming back. If all you post is information about your business, products and services, your readers might get bored and lose interest in your blog. It will be great if you can find other local bloggers and offer them guest-posting opportunities on your blog, this adds a little bit of extra flavour to your blog.

Always ask for feedback. Engagement is vital with local audiences. Ask your audience what they want and how you can make their experience better and improve your content and service. This engagement has the potential not only to make things more interesting for the readers but also to make the posts more relevant to the search engines thus yielding better ranking in search results.

The importance of an automated mailing system

In all forms of business and human engagement, time is a major challenge. One of the greatest strategies to overcome this challenge is making use of automated email systems. An automated mailing system aims at sending out routine messages or responses to clients; thus saving the time that would have been expended in sending the message to every client individually. These aims at increasing website traffic, saving time and improving efficiency and profit.

Automated mailing systems lead to an increase in site visits and readership. It also keeps your readers well informed. For offline businesses, on the other hand, it increases the number of physical visits to your business and thus increases sales of your products and services.

Chapter 24

Importance of follow-up and feedback

In this section, an analogy will be used to explain the importance of follow-up and constant communication with your clients.

In a lot of countries, power company operations are regulated by the government. What this means in essence, is that you have no choice who you purchase electricity from, you have to get it from the company that has the power facilities in your area. This is referred to as "regulated monopolies."

The implication of this situation is that no matter how upset you get with the power company; there is little or nothing that you can do about it, as your choice is virtually limited. All you can practically do is, either decide to go without electricity altogether or keep buying from them despite the fact that you are not happy with the supplier. The fact remains that the only two times when you would probably think about the power company, are when you get your bill each month and when there is a power outage or blackout. And neither of this can be termed 'a positive experience.'

There is an example of one such company whose customer satisfaction score was incredibly high in spite of the fact that the service was extremely poor that year; the secret was follow up and keeping the customers informed and updated.

In the said year, they got hit by two of the worst hurricane seasons in history. They had recurrent hurricanes that left the majority of their customers without power for weeks. Because they had exhausted their $1 Billion Dollar Storm Re-Building Fund (power companies can't get insurance on their power lines), they had charged their customers 10-15% more on their regular bills monthly to replenish their storm rebuilding funds. To aggravate the whole situation, the cost of fuel skyrocketed during this same period, so they had to increase their customers' bills by another 30% within a few short months.

They, therefore, had to deliver bad news to their customers over and over again for a period of eighteen months. Because of all these, they were apprehensive about receiving their customer satisfaction rating, assuming it will be their worst ever.

Unbelievable Response

However, they were utterly amazed when they received the customer satisfaction scores. What they scored that year, was the best ever.

It turned out that because they were in constant communication with their customers, although the information they were dishing out to their customers by calling/emailing/faxing were bad news, the customers' perception of the quality of service actually was excellent. The customers felt that in spite of all the negative happenings, the company still had their customers' welfare and satisfaction in mind. The customers understood that what happened was not the company's fault and that they did their best to manage all the incidences. The moral of this story is that communication is essential. You must keep your customers in the loop no matter what. Customers are human beings and can be both understanding and accommodating for as long you do not keep them in the dark.

"No news is bad news"!

What does all this have to do with your business? Everything!

If customers who don't have a choice procure a service from you and are still, somehow, able to get a sense of high customer support due to increased communication, how much more impactful do you think it can be for your business? Certainly, the impact will be priceless.

Just imagine how thrilled your customers will be when they receive a notification from you, about products they can acquire at bargain prices because you are having a sale. Or you send them a message offering a new service which will meet some of their identified needs. Alternatively, you send them an email just sharing a useful tip about how to get more value from your products or service. The fact is that customers and potential customers alike want to hear from your business. You have to keep in regular contact with them and start following them up. This makes them feel appreciated and the result will be you seeing your business growing immensely.

Chapter 25

Reputation Management – What is being said about you online?

Many business owners fail to recognise how critical their online reputation is. It can make the drastic difference between increased sales and a dramatic drop in sales. Just one negative comment or review is enough to affect your online reputation dramatically. Once your reputation begins to take a decline, you are likely to see a decrease in website traffic which will have a knock-on effect on the amount of sales you would eventually generate.

If you are wondering how you can keep your online reputation in good form and keep the clients and purchases coming?

The next paragraph to be introduced will take you through some steps which will help you monitor the status of your online reputation if followed..

It is important to see what potential and existing clients see when they search for your business. To do this, simply perform a search as they would, which is to type your company name into the most popular search engine - Google. This will show you what comes up on the search results and presented to searchers about you and your business.

Continuous monitoring of your online reputation will ensure that you are alerted to any harmful content published about you. When you are aware of it, you are then able to make the necessary changes to prevent or repair the damage. You put yourself in a better position to manage your reputation and take control of the situation if you know what is being said about you online.

One of the key things to do when monitoring your reputation and notice any negative post or comment regarding your business is to act quickly. Doing this will help to minimise any adverse effect it may have on your reputation and eventually the success of your business. One negative comment can be enough to make you lose your potential clients and even your existing ones.

You should also be quick to correctly address any adverse comment or negative post on any of your social media pages. The sooner you act to rectify the situation, the less likely it is that the dissatisfied customer will continue to post additional comments. However, if you choose to avoid the situation and hope it will go away or resolve itself, then you give the customer more of an incentive to keep posting more negative comments. This can indeed, have a dramatically damaging effect on your online reputation.

The key, of course, is to act quickly, but it is imperative that the correct course of action is taken. There is no point in responding swiftly, but end up fueling the fire by making comments that will further aggravate the already disgruntled customer.

It is important to take the right course of action in the bid to do everything within your power to resolve the problem.

It is paramount that you take a proactive approach to your online reputation. This will work to your advantage as it will provide you with the opportunity to gain valuable insights about the type of content being published about your business and brand. The more involved you are in the process, the easier it will be to notice any newly published harmful content. Once you are aware of this content, as mentioned above, the key is to act quickly, decisively and appropriately. This action will ensure that the harmful content is taken care of and most probably replaced with positive comments and content.

Few issues can be as damaging to a business as negative comments or reviews about that business. However, if you are proactive and continue to monitor your online reputation, you will be better prepared to deal with these situations as they occur. The key to keeping your online reputation pristine is in being proactive. Be on the watch out for your business.

Chapter 26

More On Branding

Properly branding your business is one of the most important steps you have to take to market your local business successfully. Building and establishing your brand will help inform potential clients about what your company does and who you are.

One of the most vital aspects of your brand is your logo. It is what will become the face of your company and what people will associate with you and your business. Having consistency across all the platforms is essential in portraying a congruent and uniform brand.

One sure way to stand out from your competition is by properly branding your business. Branding will help set your business apart from your competitors. Your business is unique and it should be branded accordingly. This will also enable you to reach your target audience more effectively and create marketing plans focussed on your brand. Invariably what this means is that your message will be heard by those who can genuinely benefit from the products and services you have to offer.

Branding your business will also assist you in creating an emotional connection with customers. When you emotionally connect with your customers, you provide a way in which they can identify and connect with your business and product. You can achieve this objective by using a well-designed logo and marketing plan. Your logo is what will identify your business; hence the design should be something that is recognisable as your brand and thus act as the identity of your business.

Furthermore, a well-established brand is another effective way to engender trust with your target market. When potential clients think that you are a trustworthy business, then the likelihood of them purchasing your products and services is so much higher. A business that is properly branded will have a greater response from their emails, advertisements, and newsletters campaigns. As more people become interested in your brand, they will gain more confidence in the products and services that you provide. This trust can subsequently be translated to increased website traffic and eventually sales.

Your brand is not something that is only being created to serve a short-term goal. The long-term goals of your business should be one of your primary focus when you are building your brand. You have to envision the brand that you build being robust enough to survive both expansions and time but still retaining its consistency. This type of long-term marketing strategy is attractive to your existing customers as well as your prospective ones.

You should design your brand in such a way that it enhances your business while adding a sense of stability, dependability and authenticity to your business. Your brand will be used as your source of identification right now and in future years. Therefore, your brand needs to be able to inspire trust in the minds of your customers for a very long time.

Chapter 27

The 8 Basics for Marketing Your Business Online

Marketing your business online takes a great deal of planning, commitment and the decision to use the tools available efficiently and maximally. Given the vast number of online promotion methods that businesses are accessible to, in today's market, it is paramount to ensure that only the appropriate tools are used and used effectively to keep your business on the right track to success.

To have you achieve this feat for your business, below is a list of eight essentials to look out for as you market your business on the internet.

Essentials to keep in mind as you venture to market your business online:-

- **Essential 1**

It is crucial to invest some time in carefully planning out the best strategies and answering some relevant questions before commencing the online campaign.

Below are some pertinent questions that need answers:-

What is your goal?
What are your desired benefits?
How much time can the business dedicate to research and analysis?

One foolproof strategy is to begin with the basics, then develop and expand as you go along.

- **Essential 2**

Regularly check to ascertain that your website and contact information on all online searches are accurate and up to date. Check all your links and backlinks to ensure that they are valid and functioning. Remove the ones that aren't working so that you get constant traffic, unhindered by bugs.

- **Essential 3**

Take your online plan and the maintenance seriously (even like a full-fledged legitimate department in your business empire). Put concrete structures in place to appropriately monitor data and make needed adjustments on a consistent basis. Regular 'department meetings' can be he held to identify and resolve issues.

Assuming that automation and follow-ups will happen on their own will cause huge mistakes and could create missteps and missed opportunities.

- **Essential 4**

Be consistent in your communication with your contacts. Make sure that clients hear from you. Share the most pertinent information about your business and any important event or promotion that might be of benefit to them. Share as many of business success stories as possible as well as any impending changes that may be on the horizon. Inform your clients about your milestones too; this can be an indication that you appreciate them for trusting in your business and staying with you.

- **Essential 5**

It is imperative that your company's mission has a prominent position. Always make sure that your content, as well as other writings, align with your mission. Make sure that there is a high awareness of your mission by any agencies you sub-contract any of your marketing services to. Have an approval process in place for any content that is going to be posted.

- **Essential 6**

Make the most use of social media. The reality is that although good news travels fast, bad news travels faster. Ensure that the messages and social connection opportunities are positive reflections of your business. You can do this by finding clients who are willing to write positive reviews and comments on pages like Facebook and Google+.

- **Essential 7**

Make sure that your customers have an avenue to give feedback and suggestions. They will feel listened to, respected and appreciated and will eventually become loyal advocates of your company and brand.

- **Essential 8**

Tap into the emotions and life of your clients by celebrating special dates such as their birthdays and anniversaries with them. You can also remind them as a form of appreciation of the day of their first visit and purchase from you. The possibilities are endless, use the data you have on your clients to select from the vast number of opportunities available to appreciate your customers and increase their confidence in you and your business.

Chapter 28

Useful Social Media Tools and Resources

Social Media Tools for Facebook

Agora Pulse
http://www.agorapulse.com
This is a social media management platform that offers solutions for Facebook as well as other platforms such as Twitter, Instagram, LinkedIn, Google+ and Youtube.

Ecwid
https://www.ecwid.com/
Ecwid is a shopping cart tool that allows you to add an online store to Facebook and any other social media site.

DrumUp
https://drumup.io
This is mostly focused on automating content strategy and marketing efforts.

Socialoomph
https://www.socialoomph.com/
This tool will help boost your social media productivity.

ShortStack
http://www.shortstack.com/
This is a self-service platform will help with creating engaging social media campaigns.

TabSite
https://www.tabsite.com
You can use this tools to create a variety of engagement tools, like contests, coupons and promotions.

Hootsuite
http://www.hootsuite.com
This is a social media management tool that can be used for every social media platform available at the moment. Hootsuite helps with engaging with followers and publishing new content on Facebook as well as a host of other things

EdgeRank Checker
https://www.socialbakers.com/edgerankchecker/
This can be used to provide a complete overview and analysis of your Facebook page

Facebook Page Barometer
http://barometer.agorapulse.com/
This tool from will deliver stats on reach, engagement, feedback of your Facebook Page and compares the results to results of pages with a similar amount of fans.

AgoraPulse Contest
http://contest.agorapulse.com/
This is another cool tool from AgoraPulse, is this contest app, it lets you connect your Facebook pages and try out three different types of contest to reward those who engage with you.

Conversation Score
http://cscore.recommend.ly/
You can easily find out any fan page's influence, engagement and performance by simply entering the page URL into the Conversation Score tool.

Buffer
https://www.buffer.com
This platform that allows you to manage all your pages and accounts from the same place.
It is easy to use.

Facebook Ads Compass
https://adespresso.com/academy/free-tools/compass/#
Facebook Ads Compass from AdEspresso is a free report that analyses your Facebook Ads campaign so you can discover what is working and what isn't.

Headline Analyzer
http://coschedule.com/headline-analyzer
Headline Analyzer from CoSchedule scores your overall headline quality and rate its ability to result in social shares, increased traffic, and search-engine-optimisation value. It will also offer suggestions about how to improve a generic headline.

Share
https://sumome.com/app/share
Share is from SumoMe and it allows you to add buttons over 16 networks and services to your content. This helps your readers to easily share your posts.

Oktopost
http://www.oktopost.com/
This is a business-to-business (B2B) social media management platform.

Socialbakers Analytics
https://www.socialbakers.com/edgerankchecker
This provides a thorough analytics for Facebook as well as other social media platforms.

Post Planner

https://www.postplanner.com/

This tool helps users find the most engaging content for their specific field and helps them schedule posts for the perfect time.

NetworkedBlogs.

http://www.networkedblogs.com

This helps you to automatically update your Facebook and Twitter accounts with your latest post.

Polldaddy

https://polldaddy.com

This tool can be used to create surveys and polls to engage your Facebook followers.

Pagemodo

https://www.pagemodo.com/

This platform helps users to create a Facebook social media presence right from scratch and also provides the necessary tools for growth in the long term.

LikeAlyzer

http://likealyzer.com/

This provides you with an analysis of whatever Facebook page you want, this includes analytics information and Facebook statistics.

Qwaya

http://www.qwaya.com

This is a Facebook ads manager tool which provides multiple key functions.

Driftrock

https://www.driftrock.com/

This is an ad campaign manager for Facebook, among other things it ensures that your ads are displayed during the best time windows.

Social Media Tools for Twitter

ManageFlitter

https://www.manageflitter.com

One of the main features of this tool is the Powerpost which schedules post automatically for optimum visibility and engagement.

SocialOomph

http://www.socialoomph.com

This has a number of tools that you can use to automate your Twitter profile. Some of the features are as follows:

- Auto send DM to new followers
- Automatic follow new followers
- Send recurring tweets
- Delete all DM or Tweets
- RSS Feed to tweet

Audiense

http://www.audiense.com

This tool has features that will help users make most out of your Twitter account. You can use this tool to easily bulk follow, unfollow & find other twitter users.

Tweriod

www.tweriod.com

This is a great tool to help you get to know your followers better. You can use the information to schedule your tweets at the time that they are most active. This will engender better engagement.

Tweepi

http://www.Tweepi.com

This tool provides you with information about Twitter users with your relative interest that you can follow.

Twilert

http://www.twilert.com

This is Twitter's equivalent of Google Alerts. Once you set up your keywords and you will get email alerts when you or your brand gets mentioned on Twitter.

TweetChat

www.tweetchat.com

TweetChat enables users to chat individually, rather than doing it by public mentioning usinghashtags.

Commun it

www.commun.it

You can use this tool to schedule tweets and automate a number of activities, this would result in increased engagement.

GroupTweet

www.grouptweet.com

This tool allows you to engage with groups privately.

Twibes

http://www.twibes.com/

Twibes is a great tool for building effective connections with groups based on different interests and topics.

TweetStats

http://www.tweetstats.com

This is a fantastic tool to help you keep track of your tweets.

TweetReach

http://www.tweetreach.com

This is a great tool that will let you know how far your tweet has travelled so you know the true reach of your tweets.

Klout

www.klout.com

This tool helps you keep track of all your social media accounts and helps keep track of your influence online.

TwtQpon

http://www.twtqpon.com

TwtQpon is a tool that allows you to offer coupons for products to people who tweet about them.

TwtPoll

www.twtpoll.com

This can be used for gathering feedback from your loyal followers by creating social media surveys that could be posted directly to Facebook or Twitter.

Tweetdeck

https://tweetdeck.twitter.com/

This tool is like your personal browser that helps you go through Twitter quickly.

Storm it

http://nfnlabs.in/stormit

Storm is a particularly great app for those who write long tweets (longer than 140 characters) because it automatically chops them up and shares them as individual tweets.

CircleCount

http://www.circlecount.com/

Use this tool to track followers and analyse your shares.

Buffer

https://bufferapp.com/

Use tool to optimise online social media sharing and save time.

KnowEm

http://knowem.com/

Tool to check for the use of your brand, product, personal name or username instantly on over 500 popular and emerging social media websites.

RowFeeder
https://rowfeeder.com/
Tool for social media monitoring and analysis.

Social Authority
https://followerwonk.com/social-authority
Use tool to find out how much social authority your followers and the people you want to connect with have.

Social Crawlytics
https://socialcrawlytics.com/
Use tool to carry out research of competitors' most-shared content.

General Social Media Tools

Shared Count
http://www.sharedcount.com/
Use tool to find out the content that has been shared socially across the major platforms

Social Mention
http://www.socialmention.com/
This provides real-time social media search and analysis.

Buffer
www.buffer.com
This provides great insights that helps you make the most of your social media marketing activities.

Nuvi
www.nuvi.com
This is an excellent tool for social media data visualisations. It helps simplify social media data reporting and monitoring.

Edgar
www.meetedgar.com
This schedules content by categories and recycles older updates in order to maintain engagement and widen social reach.

Post Planner
www.postplanner.com
This helps to identify which content is best for your audience. Users are able to browse feeds that Post Planner recommends to discover the new content.

CoSchedule
www.coschedule.com
This is actually a marketing calendar that links and manages all of your platforms. This helps you to plan, promote and execute all your social media strategies with one tool.

Sprout Social

www.sproutsocial.com

This a social media management platform that helps streamline social engagement.

Later

http://later.com/

This is a fantastic Instagram post scheduling app. It has features such as an intuitive calendar view, bulk uploading, and a search function.

Tweetdeck

https://tweetdeck.twitter.com/

Tweetdeck was acquired by Twitter. It is a simple tool mainly for Twitter. It organises messages, notifications and so much more.

Canva

https://www.canva.com/

Canva makes it pretty easy for people to create beautiful images.

Bitly

https://bitly.com

This is a URL shortener and it also lets track individual link analytics so you can gain information on your audiences and measure campaign performances.

Click to Tweet

https://clicktotweet.com

Click to Tweet makes the job of promoting, sharing and tracking content on Twitter really simple.

Curalate

https://www.curalate.com/

Curalate (formerly Like2Buy) lets people make their Instagram feeds more interactive.

Have2HaveIt
https://have2have.it/
This is another Instagram platform

Yotpo
https://www.yotpo.com/
It is a marketing tool that helps generate real reviews for brands.

Pocket
https://getpocket.com/
Pocket is a tool that allows users to save links for later. It's a really useful tool.

Facebook Live
https://live.fb.com/
Facebook Live allows people and companies alike to connect with their audiences.

Audiense
https://audiense.com/
Audiense (formerly SocialBro) provides a wealth of social media insights.

Mention
https://mention.com/
This is one of the best tools to use in monitoring your brand across the web and social media.

Klout
https://klout.com/
This tool analyses your Klout Score – this is ameasure of your influence on social media.

SocialRank
https://socialrank.com/
SocialRank is a tool that helps users in identify, organise and manage followers on Twitter and Instagram.

Website Tools

Sitemap Generators
https://www.xml-sitemaps.com/
Use this tool to generate sitemaps
http://www.removeem.com/ratios.php
Use this tool to discover links which Google might not be happy with and change them.

Website review
https://www.woorank.com
Get a review of any website with this tool, it shows the current score for your website along with a report emphasising what you're doing correctly and what you're not doing yet.

PageSpeed Insights
http://developers.google.com/speed/pagespeed/insights/
Discover the speed of webpages on all devices using this tool and also receive suggestions for improvement.

Google Position Checker Tool
https://www.searchenginegenie.com/google-rank- checker.html
Use this tool to query Google's search engines ranking position.

Site Analyser
http://www.site-analyzer.com/
Analyse website with this tool.

BuiltWith
http://builtwith.com/
Use tool to ascertain what technology any website was built with.

Link Building Tools http://tools.buzzstream.com/link-building
Use tools for link building.

Copyscape
http://www.copyscape.com/
This helps to check for plagiarism duplicate-content.

Domain Hunter Plus
http://domainhunterplus.com/
This helps you discover important broken links and also informs you if the links point to an available domain.

Robots.txt Checker
http://tools.seobook.com/robots-txt/analyzer/
Discover errors in robots.txt files with this tool.

Siteliner
http://www.siteliner.com/
Use tool to check duplicate content, broken links, XML sitemap, internal page rank and more.

Backlinks
http://www.openlinkprofiler.org/
Get the freshest backlinks with this tool.

Gtmetrix
http://gtmetrix.com/
This is a tool for measuring the speed of a website.

Free Google penalty checker
http://fruition.net/google-penalty-checker-tool/
Tool to keep up with Google changes so as to avoid Google penalties.

Sitemap inspector
http://sitemapinspector.com/
Validate your sitemap and get a new one free from errors

Sitemap generator http://www.sitemapdoc.com/ Generate free sitemaps with this tool.

Linkstant
http://www.linkstant.com/
This tool alerts you immediately someone links to your website.

MozCast
http://mozcast.com/
This informs you of daily google algorithm changes.

Panguin Tool
http://www.barracuda-digital.co.uk/panguin-tool/
This tool enables you to see if Google Algorithm updates have impacted you.
Pingdom http://tools.pingdom.com/fpt/
Tool to test loading time of webpages and discover any bottlenecks.

Piwik
http://piwik.org/
This tool gives you valuable insights about visitors' to your website and your marketing campaigns.

GA Checker
http://www.gachecker.com/
This tool checks your entire site for missing Google Analytics or AdWords code with one click.

Sitebeam
http://sitebeam.net/
Compare and rank websites with this tool.

Robots.txt Checker
http://tool.motoricerca.info/robots-checker.phtml
This tool analyses the syntax of a robots.txt file to see if its format is valid.

Schema Creator
http://schema-creator.org/
The easiest way to create HTML with schema.org microdata

Lipperhey
http://links.lipperhey.com/
Tool to analyse existing incoming links to your website, allows comparison to specific competitors and gives recommendation about websites to get links for your site.

Web Me Up
http://webmeup.com/
Tool to clean-up your backlink profile, execute a link audit or steal a competitor's backlink secrets.

Serp Fox
http://serpfox.com/
Tool to monitor your search engine rankings over multiple time frames and plot graphs.

Cuterank
http://cuterank.net/
Check and track your keyword rankings on multiple search engines.

Wayback Machine http://archive.org/web/web.php
Competitive Intelligence
This tool allows you to see the history of your competitor's site and track important changes.

WebPagetest
http://www.webpagetest.org/
Run a free website speed test and get suggestions for improving performance.

Xenu's Link Sleuth
http://home.snafu.de/tilman/xenulink.html
This helps you find broken links.

XML-Sitemaps.com
http://www.xml-sitemaps.com/
Tool for creating sitemaps.

URI Valet
http://urivalet.com/
This is a tool for investigating server headers.

Nibbler
http://nibbler.silktide.com/
Tool for testing websites

Google Algorithm Updates
https://www.analytics-toolkit.com/google-algorithm-updates/
Lets you instantly check whether your website has been hit by a Penguin, Panda, Hummingbird or another algorithm update.

Ahrefs
https://ahrefs.com/
A powerful tool for checking links.

CloudFlare
https://www.cloudflare.com/
Tool for supercharging your website and for making it more secure.

Algoroo
http://algoroo.com/
Google algorithm tracking tool, thislets you visualise various Google updates on a chart.

Site scan
http://www.site-scan.com/eng/site-scan/start.php
Google sitemaps generator

PageRank
http://www.site-scan.com/eng/show_pagerank.php
Tool to Check your Google PageRank

AnalogX LinkExaminer
http://www.analogx.com/contents/download/Network/lnkex
am/Freeware.htm
Checks links and identifies pages with high similarity to other pages.

Site Condor
sitecondor.com/app/#/pagechecks/create
Tool that lets you track and understand content, visual, and performance changes over time.

Media4x
http://media4x.com
A tool for compressing your images so that your website loads faster.

Open Link Profiler
http://openlinkprofiler.org/
Tool to get in-depth analysis of the freshest live backlinks.

Similar Page Checker
http://www.webconfs.com/similar-page-checker.php
Use tool to check for duplicate content.

Onestatfree
http://www.onestatfree.com/
Hit counter tool

Go Stats
http://gostats.com/
Hit Counter and Web Analytics

Whitespark Local Citation Finder
https://www.whitespark.ca/local-citation-finder/
Tool to discover local citations.

Search Metrics
http://suite.searchmetrics.com/en/research
Domain and backlink profile analysis as many other functions.

QuickSprout Website Analyzer
http://www.quicksprout.com/
Use for full analysis of your website

nTopic
http://www.ntopic.org/
Tool to analyse content for relevancy and get suggestions to improve it.

Optimizely
https://www.optimizely.com/
Optimisation platform for websites and mobile apps.

StatCounter
http://statcounter.com/
Useful tool for Website Visitor Analysis.

SimilarWeb
http://www.similarweb.com/

Google Snippet Preview
http://snippetoptimizer.net/
Tool that assists with visualisation and optimisation of what is displayed to web users.

W3 Webtools
http://w3webtools.com
A variety of useful SEO tools.

Responsinator
http://responsetester.appspot.com/
Tool to check for correct server response codes.

Keyword Tools

Related Keywords Finder
http://tools.seochat.com/tools/related-keywords-tool/
Use this tool to get a list of related keywords.

Spying on your competitors.
http://www.spyfu.com/
Use tool to track your competitors' most profitable keywords and Ads

Competition keyword research tool
http://www.semrush.com/
Use tool to gather information about the keywords your competition are bidding on.

Gather Data about competitors
http://www.ispionage.com/
See ads that competitors are running with accompanying ranking information

Keyword Research Tool
http://ubersuggest.org/
Use tool to research keyword ideas.

Google Keyword Planner
http://adwords.google.com/keywordplanner
Use tool for keyword research

Spy On the Web
http://spyonweb.com/
Another spying tool.

Keyword Tool
http://keywordtool.io/
Tool to discover what web users are searching for.

Wordtracker
http://www.wordtracker.com/
Keyword Research Tool

Live Keyword Analysis
http://www.live-keyword-analysis.com/
Keyword density analysis

Google Trends
http://www.google.com/trends/
Great tool to discover what is trending on Google to help with keyword research.

SEO Tools

Bing Webmaster Tools
http://www.bing.com/toolbox/webmaster
Use these various tools and resources to ultimately drive more traffic to website.

SEO Audit for domain
http://www.seoptimer.com/
Use this tool to conduct a website review and SEO audit.

SEO Toolbar
http://tools.seobook.com/seo-toolbar/
The SEO Toolbar puts a huge amount of information at your disposal including backlinks and competitive research.

SEO Tools for Excel
http://nielsbosma.se/projects/seotools/
Niels Bosma's SEO Tools for Excel

SEO Gadget
http://builtvisible.com/seogadget-for-excel/
This tool helps you gather backlink data and other valuable information.

SEO Quake
http://www.seoquake.com/
Great analytic SEO tool for Firefox, Chrome and Opera browsers.

Google Analytics
http://www.google.com/analytics/
Analytics tools

Serps
https://serps.com/tools/rank_checker
Keyword Rank Checker & SERP Checker
Google Map Maker
http://www.google.com/mapmaker
The tool that can be used to contribute to public map information.

Google Public Data
http://www.google.com/publicdata/directory
This can be used to conduct content research and more.

Google SERP Snippet Optimization Tool
http://www.seomofo.com/snippet-optimizer.html
Tool to see how your snippet could show up in Google's search results.

Google Webmaster
http://www.google.com/webmasters/
A variety of tools available here for SEO.

SEOCrawler
https://seocrawler.co/
This tool can be used to check the health of your websites or competitors sites and to research content ideas by your competitors.

Rank Checker for Firefox.
http://tools.seobook.com/firefox/rank-checker/
Free Search Engine Ranking Checking Tool for Firefox

Visual SEO Studio.
http://visual-seo.com/
This tool makes complex SEO tasks quick and easy.

Majestic SEO
http://www.majesticseo.com/
Tool for Link Research and Link Building.

MozBar
http://moz.com/tools/seo-toolbar
Tools for accessing important SEO metrics, it also can be used to see how difficult it is to rank for a given keyword and many other functions.

FatRank by FatJoe,
http://fatjoe.co/fat-rank/
Keyword Rank Checker

Wordstream
http://www.wordstream.com/free-keyword-tools

Free Keyword Tools

Keyword Eye
http://www.keywordeye.com/
Keyword Research Tool.

Seer Toolbox
http://toolbox.seerinteractive.com/
This an all-in-one toolbox made for SEOs

Yoast WordPress SEO Plugin
http://yoast.com/wordpress/seo/
Optimise your WordPress site with this one plugin

CognitiveSEO (free and paid) – multitool
http://www.cognitiveseo.com/
Tool for Backlink Analysis, Content Audit and Rank Tracking.

Microsoft SEO Toolkit
http://www.microsoft.com/web/seo/
The SEO Toolkit gives detailed analysis and search engine friendly suggestions to help improve the relevance of your website in search results.

Raven
http://raventools.com/
A variety of SEO and research tools.

51 Blocks
http://www.51blocks.com/tools/
This offers a variety of local SEO tools.

SEO Browser
http://browseo.net./
This allows you to view any webpage without distractions caused by styles. It also highlights parts of a page that are relevant for SEO.

SEO Web Page Analyzer
http://www.seowebpageanalyzer.com/
This tool breaks down the structure and content of your web page and assesses both the build and content quality from an accessibility, usability and search engine point of view.

SEO bin
http://seobin.org/
This free SEO tool will help you optimise title tags and tweak meta description tags.

Screaming Frog
http://www.screamingfrog.co.uk/
This tool spiders websites' links, images, CSS, script and apps from an SEO perspective.

Image SEO Tool
http://www.feedthebot.com/tools/
Checks image name, alt attribute, and dimensions. It gives alerts if a potential problem is discovered.

SEO Site Check up
http://seositecheckup.com/
Tool to audit and get the score for your website.

Blekko
http://blekko.com/
A search engine/SEO tool that gets website insights by performing SEO specific queries.

Monitoring Tools

1. **Google Alerts**
When you set up Google alerts you will basically receive email alerts each time anyone mentions your company or whatever name you are tracking. Google Alerts lets you set up keyword searches for your company name or even your competition, if you want to keep tabs on what they are doing. You will receive instant updates through email daily or weekly directly into your inbox or through an RSS feed.
It is extremely easy to set up. Simply go to www.google.com/alerts and fill out your company name search query. You can select which type of content you are looking for, your preferred update frequency and quantity. Google Alerts will update you and keep you informed about new mentions on the web.
Make sure you add a very specific search query and select the appropriate channel; otherwise you will end up receiving too many alerts in your email inbox.
See below:
This is where your preferences will be selected, such as:
How Often – You can choose - once per day, once per week, or as-it-happens, whatever suits you best. Bear in mind that these alerts

will be sent into the Google email account linked to your Alerts.
Sources – Select what you want to be alerted about, be it news, videos, etc. If you want to be notified about everything, it is recommended that you choose the "Automatic" option.
Language and Region – This is quite clear, input your preferred language and region for the alert.
How Many – Indicate "Only the best results" if you are after high quality, related terms. Select "All results" if that is your preference, this will include low quality ones.
Deliver To – You choose where you want to view your alerts either through RSS feed or your linked Google email account.
Alert Suggestions –Under the "Alert suggestions" section, Google will bring up other suggestions, simply click on the "+" next to them if you want to add them and they will be added to your alert list.
Once all of your preferences have been chosen, you can click on the "Create Alert" button at the bottom.

2. Tweet Alarm

Tweet Alarm is a great automatic monitoring system to use keep updated on what happens on Twitter. Tweet alarm will alert you by send you email whenever someone tweets about your brand, products or anything that interests you. Registration is required.

3. TweetBeep

TweetBeep works in a similar manner to Google Alerts, the only difference being that it monitors your reputation exclusively on Twitter. A free version of Tweetbeep will send you updates every hour whenever you are mentioned on Twitter.

4. HootSuite

HootSuite is a popular tool that can be used for enhancing and managing multiple social media accounts such as Facebook, Twitter, MySpace, Google+ Pages, LinkedIn, WordPress, Foursquare etc from one location. HootSuite eradicates the time consuming element involved in managing several social media accounts. It helps in monitoring what is being said about you and enables you to give immediate responses. It also amongst a number of other benefits makes it possible for you to schedule messages in advance from all your social media channels and post updates or respond directly.

5. Social Mention

What Social Mention does according to the website [1] is that, "it allows you to easily track and measure what people are saying about you, your company, a new product, or any topic across the web's social media landscape in real-time. Social Mention monitors 100+ social media properties directly including: Twitter, Facebook, FriendFeed, YouTube, Digg, Google etc."

Social Mention enables you to see whether your company started off any dialogues on social media, what the author/mention ratio is, what your influence score is and people's sentiment.

It assists in tracking blogs, blog comments, mainstream news, Twitter, images, audio and video.

6. Mention

This is an iPhone and Android app that allows you to set up alerts for your company, brand, keywords, and your competition. 'Mention' has a number of features, it allows you to "connect social accounts to your alerts and react without leaving the application". In addition it helps you "monitor millions of sources in 42 languages and make sure you're not missing anything published on social networks, news sites, forums, blogs or any web page". [2]

7. Whos Talkin

This is a social media search tool that displays what is being said about you on different social networks. It is a simple tool to use, you basically enter the name of your company, click search and wait for the results. Whos Talkin will not help you manage the results, but will let you know pretty quickly what is being said about you online. You now have to make a decision on what you do with the results.

8. Cyfe

Cyfe is an all-in-one dashboard software that helps you monitor and analyze data scattered across all your online services like Google Analytics, Salesforce, AdSense, MailChimp, Facebook, WordPress and more from one single location in real-time

9. Technorati

This is one of the main blog search engine directories. You can use this for blog posts monitoring as well as to search for keywords connected to your company and even your competition.

10. "Addictomatic searches the best live sites on the web for the latest news, blog posts, videos and images. It's the perfect tool to keep up with the hottest topics, perform ego searches and feed your addiction for what's up, what's now or what other people are feeding on". [3]

This tool summarises on one page how your brand is being perceived on a variety of social media platforms.

11. Pin Alerts

Pin Alerts will send emails to inform you when your website gets a new pin on Pinterest. This service can be set up very quickly and easily. Once set up automatic notifications will be sent this is great as users do not have to continuously monitor the pins. The users dictate how often they want to receive the email alerts, be it in real time as it happens, daily or weekly. The emails will include a link to the latest pins and description. Pin Alerts has the ability to track more than one domain.

12. Topsy

This is a great social analytics tool that you can use to scan the internet to find mentions of your company name, product, competition etc. The main thing that makes this tool different from the other monitoring tools is that it has indexed every single tweet that has ever been tweeted.

Topsy does not only let you find out about what is being said about you online, but also reveal trending topics that you can include on your dashboard.

13. If This Then That

If This Then That, is a fairly new social media tool that enables you to "put the internet to work for you". It helps you connect with numerous social media platforms and devices, so that you generate so-called "recipes", this will help you get notifications. "Most Personal Recipes check for new Trigger data every 15 minutes, some are even faster". In addition you can choose one of the public recipes and reproduce what some other people are doing on this platform.

14. Netvibes

Netvibes is an all-in-one dashboard intelligence platform that you can use for social media monitoring in real-time. You do not have to be online to read feeds, this can be done anywhere including offline. Netvibes can be used on different devices such as iPhone, iPad, Android, desktop browser etc.

15. Image Raider

Image Raider is a tool that you can use to detect if someone is using your photo online. All you do is upload your photo on Image Raider and it will conduct a reverse image search and let you know if there are people talking about you using your pictures without saying your name. It will also enable you discover if your photos have been stolen or altered.

16. Icerocket

Icerocket is a tool that you can use to monitor mentions of your company online be it on blogs, Facebook and Twitter. It is relatively easy to use all you do is type what you want monitored into the search bar and the result will be delivered on one page. You can use it to search multiple social platforms such as blogs, Facebook or Twitter either individually or all at the same time.

17. BackTweets

This tool tracks the number of people talking about you, identifies who is talking and what they're saying. It helps both individuals and companies measure their Twitter reach in quantity and quality by displaying how often a link was tweeted including the actual tweet that was made.

18. CustomScoop

This provides all-in-one news and social media monitoring. You can access different types of services, for instance a 24/7 automated dashboard or if your preference is a sophisticated human analysis you can get that too. CustomScoop provides customised solutions that will meet your needs.

References

[1] http://socialmention.com/about/
[2] https://en.mention.com/features
[3]http://addictomatic.com/about

Summing it all up

We specialise in helping local organisations get things set up to succeed online, and we're here, ready to help.
Take a look at our websites at:
www.aceresultsmarketing.com
www.reputationmaven.com
Online Consultancy, bespoke web design and SEO services.

Services We Can Offer Businesses

Majority of people these days use search engines like Google to look for everything including local services and products.
The best way for the thousands of people looking for the products or services you provide is by finding you on first page Google.
We can help your business get found on the internet where people are looking: Google, Yahoo!, Bing, Ask, and other search engines. That means more potential visitors to your website, more phone calls, and more people physically walking through your door and buying from you online...

ADDITIONAL SERVICES WE PROVIDE

Mobile Marketing
Mobile Websites Mobile Coupons Text Marketing Click To Call

Mobile Apps

On-Page Optimisation
Keyword Research
Title Tag Optimisation
Image & Hyperlink Optimization
Header Tag Optimisation

Local Search

Website Optimisation

Local Search Engine Submission
Customer Review Submission
Updating Pages for Local Search

Content Optimisation

Website Content Writing
Blog Writing Article Writing Press Release

Web 2.0 and Social Media Optimisation

Social Bookmarking
Blog Submission
Press Release Submission
Article Submissio
PowerPoint Presentation Submission
Video Submission
Photo Sharing
RSS Feeds Link Development
Manual Link
Requests to Related Sites

Reporting
Website SEO Audits
Google Analytics (Statistics)
Current Performance
Monthly SEO Report

Writing
Social Media Marketing
Video Marketing
Online Reputation Management
Livestreaming Podcasting

One Way Links from Directory Submissions

Other Activities

Google, Yahoo & MSN Sitemap Creation

First Page Google Service

Made in United States
North Haven, CT
04 November 2026

21765296R00085